REFORMING THE MONASTERY

NML NEW MONASTIC LIBRARY
Resources for Radical Discipleship

For over a millennium, if Christians wanted to read theology, practice Christian spirituality, or study the Bible, they went to the monastery to do so. There, people who inhabited the tradition and prayed the prayers of the church also copied manuscripts and offered fresh reflections about living the gospel in a new era. Two thousand years after the birth of the church, a new monastic movement is stirring in North America. In keeping with ancient tradition, new monastics study the classics of Christian reflection and are beginning to offer some reflections for a new era. The New Monastic Library includes reflections from new monastics as well as classic monastic resources unavailable elsewhere.

Series Editor: Jonathan Wilson-Hartgrove

VOL. 2: *Inhabiting the Church: Biblical Wisdom for a New Monasticism*, by Jon R. Stock, Tim Otto, and Jonathan Wilson-Hartgrove

VOL. 3: *Community of the Transfiguration: The Journey of a New Monastic Community*, by Paul R. Dekar

VOL. 4: *"Follow Me": A History of Christian Intentionality*, by Ivan J. Kauffman

VOL. 5: *Longing for Spring: A New Vision for Wesleyan Community*, by Elaine A. Heath and Scott T. Kisker

VOL. 6: *Living Faithfully in a Fragmented World, Second Edition: From After Virtue to a New Monasticism*, by Jonathan R. Wilson

VOL. 7: *Plunging into the Kingdom Way: Practicing the Shared Strokes of Community, Hospitality, Justice, and Confession*, by Tim Dickau

VOL. 8: *Against the Tide, Towards the Kingdom*, by Jenny and Justin Duckworth

VOL. 9: *Thomas Merton: Twentieth-Century Wisdom for Twenty-First-Century Living*, by Paul R. Dekar

VOL. 10: *Being Church: Reflections on How to Live as the People of God*, by John F. Alexander

VOL. 11: *A Glimpse of the Kingdom in Academia: Academic Formation as Radical Discipleship*, by Irene Alexander

VOL. 13: *A Fresh Wind Blowing: Living in God's New Pentecost*, by Steve Harper

Reforming the
MONASTERY

Protestant Theologies of the Religious Life

GREG PETERS

CASCADE Books • Eugene, Oregon

REFORMING THE MONASTERY
Protestant Theologies of the Religious Life

New Monastic Library: Resources for Radical Discipleship 12

Copyright © 2014 Greg Peters. All rights reserved. Except for brief quotations in critical publications or reviews, no part of this book may be reproduced in any manner without prior written permission from the publisher. Write: Permissions, Wipf and Stock Publishers, 199 W. 8th Ave., Suite 3, Eugene, OR 97401.

Cascade Books
An Imprint of Wipf and Stock Publishers
199 W. 8th Ave., Suite 3
Eugene, OR 97401

www.wipfandstock.com

ISBN 13: 978-1-60608-173-0

Cataloging-in-Publication data:

Peters, Greg, 1971–

    Reforming the monastery : Protestant theologies of the religious life / Greg Peters.

    x + 168 p.; 23 cm—Includes bibliographical references and index.

    ISBN 13: 978-1-60608-173-0

    New Monastic Library: Resources for Radical Discipleship 12

    1. Monasticism and religious orders, Protestant. 2. Christian communities. 3. Protestantism. I. Title. II. Series.

BV4405 .P48 2014

Manufactured in the USA.

To my parents, Carson and Gloria Peters,
for the many years of love and encouragement
that have made my life so rich.
Thank you for setting me on such a
wonderful path.

CONTENTS

Acknowledgments ix
Introduction 1
1 The Protestant Reformers 19
2 The Anglican Tradition 53
3 Karl Barth and Dietrich Bonhoeffer 91
4 Donald Bloesch and the Evangelical Tradition 127
Conclusion 153
Bibliography 155
Index 163

ACKNOWLEDGMENTS

Anyone who has written a book knows that it takes a small army of supporters to make it happen. This book is no exception. My first exposure to monasticism came by way of Denis Farkasfalvy, O.Cist., monk of Our Lady of Dallas Cistercian Monastery, and through knowing, worshipping, and studying with the monks and nuns of St. John's School of Theology in Collegeville, Minnesota, particularly Columba Stewart, O.S.B., and Mary Forman, O.S.B. I offer many thanks to Denis, Columba, and Mary for their friendship, guidance, and encouragement over the years. Though this book comes too late for him to read, I am forever grateful to the late Donald Bloesch for his writings on monasticism and Christian community, but especially for his friendship and hospitality on a visit to Dubuque, Iowa, in 2004. As always my colleagues and students in the Torrey Honors Institute of Biola University have been good conversation partners and make teaching such a joy. I am also thankful to the administration of Biola University for their ongoing support of my research, especially to Provost David Nystrom for inviting me to present my findings at a Provost's Research Luncheon in February 2011. Behind every professor who writes a book is an assistant doing the bulk of the grunt work. Immeasurable appreciation goes to Stephanie Lewis for her assistance over the past four years. Without her this book never would have made it to print. I thank my sons, Brendan and Nathanael, for making my life so much fun. Without them I would spend too much time in my office and in my books instead of throwing baseballs, swimming, and laughing. My wife, Christina, continues to enthusiastically support my preoccupation with monasticism. Without her twenty years of support I doubt that I would be where I am today. Finally, I would like to honor my parents, Carson and Gloria Peters, by dedicating this book to them in gratefulness for their unending love and encouragement.

Introduction

As I was researching and preparing to write this book, I was asked on more than one occasion: you can write a whole book on Protestant theologies of monasticism? Do Protestants really have something to say about the monastic life? The answer, of course, is "Yes!"—and it is my goal in this book to explicate the range of what select Protestant theologians have said about monasticism. The typical, if I am allowed to generalize, response from many Protestants to the institution of monasticism is akin to words penned by the great Scottish writer Robert Louis Stevenson. After rejecting his parents' Presbyterianism, Stevenson, in his *Travels with a Donkey in the Cevennes*, writes about his brief stay in 1878 at the French Cistercian-Trappist community of Our Lady of the Snows. He tells us that he meets two other guests, a French "country parish priest" and an "old soldier" who had recently entered the monastery as a novice. After talking one evening about politics, "this couple found out I was a heretic. I supposed I had misled them by some admiring expressions as to the monastic life around us; and it was only by a point-blank question that the truth came out." The two men immediately called for Stevenson's conversion, though the writer maintained that he believed that in the end all would be received by the "undiscriminating Friend and Father." This so surprised the priest and the soldier that they asked Stevenson to visit with the monastery's superior. At that point, "in came one of the monks, a little brown fellow, as lively as a grig . . . who threw himself at once into the contention, but in a milder and more persuasive vein." The attempted evangelization continued that evening until Stevenson "grew annoyed beyond endurance." Finally, the priest assured Stevenson that he only had an interest in his soul. Stevenson responded, "And there ended my conversion." Sometime after this visit and episode, Stevenson wrote a poem titled "Our Lady of the Snows." It is in

1

Reforming the Monastery

this poem where we really see Stevenson's thought regarding monasticism. Notice, in particular, those words that I have italicized:

> Out of the sun, out of the blast,
> Out of the world, alone I passed
> Across the moor and through the wood
> To where the monastery stood.
> There neither lute nor breathing fife,
> Nor rumour of the world of life,
> Nor confidences low and dear,
> Shall strike the meditative ear.
> *Aloof*, *unhelpful*, and *unkind*,
> The *prisoners* of the iron mind,
> Where nothing speaks except the bell
> The *unfraternal* brothers dwell.
> *Poor* passionate men, still clothed afresh
> With agonising folds of flesh;
> Whom the clear eyes solicit still
> To some bold output of the will,
> While fairy Fancy far before
> And musing Memory-Hold-the-door
> Now to heroic death invite
> And now uncertain fresh delight:
> O, little boots it thus to dwell
> On the remote unneighboured hill!
>
> O to be up and doing, O
> Unfearing and unshamed to go
> In all the uproar and the press
> About my human business!
> My undissuaded heart I hear
> Whisper courage in my ear.
> With voiceless calls, the ancient earth
> Summons me to a daily birth.
> Thou, O my love, ye, O my friends—
> The gist of life, the end of ends—
> To laugh, to love, to live, to die,
> Ye call me by the ear and eye!

Introduction

Forth from the casemate, on the plain
Where honour has the world to gain,
Pour forth and bravely do your part,
O knights of the unshielded heart!
Forth and forever forward!—out
From prudent turret and redoubt,
And in the mellay charge amain,
To fall but yet to rise again!
Captive? ah, still, to honour bright,
A captive soldier of the right!
Or free and fighting, good with ill?
Unconquering but unconquered still!

And ye, O brethren, what if God,
When from Heav'n's top he spies abroad,
And sees on this tormented stage
The noble war of mankind rage:
What if his vivifying eye,
O monks, should pass your corner by?

For still the Lord is Lord of might;
In deeds, in deeds, he takes delight;
The plough, the spear, the laden barks,
The field, the founded city, marks;
He marks the smiler of the streets,
The singer upon garden seats;
He sees the climber in the rocks;
To him, the shepherd folds his flocks.
For those he loves that underprop
With daily virtues Heaven's top,
And bear the falling sky with ease,
Unfrowning caryatides.
Those he approves that ply the trade,
That rock the child, that wed the maid,
That with weak virtues, weaker hands,
Sow gladness on the peopled lands,

Reforming the Monastery

> And still with laughter, song and shout,
> Spin the great wheel of earth about.
>
> But ye?—O ye who linger still
> Here in your fortress on the hill,
> With placid face, with tranquil breath,
> The *unsought volunteers of death*,
> Our cheerful General on high
> With careless looks may pass you by.[1]

It is clear from this poem that Stevenson does not think highly of the Trappist monks of Our Lady of the Snows and, by extension, monasticism generally. So much so that he suggests that God might, on the last day, pass by these monks who, as the narrative of his visit indicates, were very concerned with his own conversion. Stevenson's assertion that the truly saved are the non-monastic, everyday people of the earth (traders, caregivers, and maids) allows us to judge clearly that Stevenson holds monasticism in contempt. This, I suggest, is a rather normal contention for many Protestant Christians. As the nineteenth-century Lutheran theologian Friedrich Schleiermacher once wrote, "for by their very nature religious feelings inhibit the strength of our action and invite us to calm and dedicated enjoyment; that is why the most religious people, for whom other impulses to action were lacking and who were nothing but religious, forsook the world and yielded themselves wholly to leisurely contemplation."[2] For Schleiermacher the monks and nuns of Christian history have abandoned the world to simply engage in a kind of non-active, monastic leisure. This assessment of monasticism, as it turns out, is rather charitable when compared with other Protestant assessments.

As early as the sixteenth century, during the Reformation itself, of course, Protestant Christians looked upon monks and nuns with great suspicion. Some amount of this disdain can simply be attributed to the predominant amount of anti-Roman Catholic discourse associated with the Protestant Reformation. In a sense, being critical of monasticism was part and parcel of being a Protestant, since all things Roman Catholic were to be rejected and dismissed. Michael Sattler, former Benedictine monk and prior of St. Peter's of the Black Forest monastery near Freiburg, Switzerland,

---

1. Stevenson, "Our Lady of the Snows," in *A Child's Garden of Verses*.
2. Schleiermacher, *On Religion*, 30.

Introduction

adopted Anabaptism sometime around 1523–24. Sattler was arrested by Austrian Roman Catholic authorities, and at his trial, in 1527, he stated that he left the monastery and married because of "the pomp, pride, usury, and great whoredom of the monks and priests," or so we are told in the *Martyr's Mirror*, published in 1660 by the Flemish Menonnite Thieleman Jansz van Braght. Despite this testimony there is evidence that St. Peter's monastery underwent a reform in 1519, suggesting that Sattler's monastic experience would have been better than what is attested to in many Reformation-era documents. Sattler, a well-educated monk and eventual author of the Anabaptist theological statement known as the Schleitheim Confession, was greatly influenced by his Benedictine heritage. Despite this, however, Sattler had clearly rejected the institution of monasticism, going so far as to marry a former Beguine named Margaretha, who was martyred two days after Sattler. Not only does the *Martyr's Mirror* record that Sattler rejected monasticism, but it also repeatedly berates the institution of monasticism. For example, when talking about the former Franciscan Leonhard Schiemer, the text says that he left the religious life after "beholding the impurity, wantonness, hypocrisy, and viciousness of the monks and priests." Similarly, when describing the trial of four other Anabaptist leaders in 1546, the *Martyr's Mirror* records that "four times they were brought before the authorities at Vienna, also before monks, priests and doctors, whom Christ does not in vain designate ravening wolves, of whom we are to beware." Though many more examples from the *Martyr's Mirror* could be cited, this suffices to show that the Anabaptists in general were very anti-monastic in their assessment of the cloistered religious life. Such an anti-monastic bias is not only true of those in continental Europe in the sixteenth century, but is also seen in England as well.

In his prologue to the book of Numbers, William Tyndale, Anglican reformer, martyr, and translator of the Bible into English, refers to Roman Catholics as hypocrites and heathen pagans. As well, he writes, "They have set up wilful poverty of another manner than any is commanded of God: and, the chastity of matrimony utterly defied, they have set up another wilful chastity not required of God, which they swear, vow, and profess to give God, whether he will give it them or no; and compel all their disciples thereunto, saying that it is in the power of every man's free-will to observe it, contrary to Christ and his apostle Paul." Further, "the obedience of God and man excluded, they have vowed another wilful obedience [i.e., vows to a monastic superior], condemned of all the scripture; which they will yet give God, whether he will or will not." Elsewhere, in his *Answer to Sir Thomas More's Dialogue, The Supper of the Lord*, he says that the pope teaches salvation by works and includes monasticism in his list of those false works. Similarly, in *Expositions and Notes on Sundry Portions of the Holy Scriptures, Together with the Practice of the Prelates*, Tyndale compares the prayer life of monastics with that of the New Testament Pharisees, saying that they "trusteth in the multitude of words, and in the pain and tediousness of the length of prayer . . . as ye see now to be among our friars, monks, canons and nuns." Tyndale also states that "the Pharisees were religious men, which had professed, not as now, one Dominick's [i.e., the Dominicans], the other Francis' [i.e., the Franciscans], another Bernard's rules [i.e., the Cistercians], but even to hold the very law of God. . . . They were more honourable than any sect of the monks with us, whether Observant, or Ancre [i.e., an anchorite living in solitude], or whatsoever other be had in price." In one case for Tyndale, the monks are as bad as the Pharisees, and in the latter case they are actually worse than the Pharisees. These are harsh words, considering that Jesus viewed the Pharisees as hypocrites (Matt 15:7).

In 1576, the devout Anglican William Lambarde published his *Perambulation of Kent: Containing the Description, Hystorie and Customs of that Shyre*, a history of the county of Kent. Lambarde, a lawyer by training, writes about a miracle that occurred after a "Danish" soldier killed Ælfheah (or Alphege), the early eleventh-century archbishop of Canterbury. He tells us that such "unfruitful miracles" are characteristic of "auncient monkish stories." The key word here is *monkish*, with all of its derogatory connotations. Such a judgment, it appears, is "partly informed by Lambarde's protestant suspicion of monks and their works," as we are told by J. D. Alsop in the *Oxford Dictionary of National Biography*. Similarly, the great Protestant writer John Milton, in his *Animadversions upon the Remonstrants Defence against Smectymnuus*, first published in 1642, talks about the "monkish prohibitions" of his antagonist, Anglican Bishop Joseph Hall. Again, the word *monkish* is used in a reproachful and insulting manner. In a play from 1662, written by Margaret Cavendish, one character states unapologetically, "'T'is a sain [sin] against Nature for women to be Incloystred [that is, to be nuns] . . . those women . . . are damned."

Around the time that Cavendish wrote against monks, so did John Davenant, professor of divinity at Cambridge University and Anglican bishop of Salisbury. In *An Exposition of the Epistle of St. Paul to the Colossians*, when commenting on 3:20—"Children, obey your parents in all

Introduction

things: for this is well-pleasing unto the Lord"—Davenant writes what amounts to a study of children and whether entering the monastic life as a child is a violation of Paul's admonition in Colossians. Davenant concludes his extended discussion by saying that "the perfection of a Christian life in faith and charity, not in ceremonies or monastic rules" is preferable to the Roman Catholic position on the importance of monasticism, which says that children can disobey their parents in order to enter a monastery. For, as Davenant concludes, "the work of perfection is more excellent to obey parents in the fear of God, than to subject themselves to monastic traditions."

This same sentiment is later echoed by the Puritan author Richard Adams (d. 1698), who preached a sermon sometime between 1659 and 1689 titled "What are the duties of parents and children; and how are they to be managed according to Scripture?" In this sermon, likewise preached on Colossians 3:20, Adams concludes that parents should advise their children as to their choice of "*calling*, or lasting course of life." This, he says, is against what the Roman Catholic Church teaches: "The pretension of religion in a monastic life, which the Papists urge to cajole their votaries into their unscriptural orders, as the Pharisees did Corban, (Mark vii.11–13,) saying, 'It is a gift' devoted to God . . . can be no warrant to invade the rights of parents." That Puritans like Adams would be against the institution of monasticism is not surprising. Of interest, however, is that J. I. Packer, modern scholar of Puritanism, defines Puritanism, at least in part, in relationship to monasticism. He writes,

> Puritanism was essentially a movement for church reform, pastoral renewal and evangelism, and spiritual revival; and in addition— indeed, as a direct expression of its zeal for God's honour—it was a world-view, a total Christian philosophy, in intellectual terms a Protestantised and updated medievalism, and in terms of spirituality a reformed monasticism outside the cloister and away from monkish vows.[3]

And similarly,

> Puritan piety can be fairly characterised as a reformed monasticism . . . but, like the Reformers, they believed that God calls his saints to serve him in the family, the church, and the world, rather than in any form of closed celibate society. . . . Monasticism signified to them improper and entangling vows of celibacy and

3. Packer, *Quest for Godliness*, 28.

> poverty... but in fact their aim was to "walk through the wilderness of this world" ([John] Bunyan's phrase) with as rhythmical a routine for daily life as any monastic rule had ever required, and it is illuminating to observe the parallelism.[4]

To further illustrate the extent of early modern Protestant perceptions of monasticism, we turn to a seventeenth-century English translation of a sermon by Martin Luther titled *The Signs of Christ's Coming, and of the Last Day*, published in 1661 when eschatological and millenarian concerns were at a fever pitch in England. Though the sermon was certainly translated and published for its eschatological details, it contains a stinging attack against the institution of monasticism. For example,

> ...for afflicted Consciences become so perplexed, that they know not which way to turn themselves, or what to undertake, and being placed in this doubtfulness and perplexity of mind, how easie a matter was it, for those Impostors, the Apostles of Satan, the Teachers of Humane Inventions, to perswade them any thing? And hereupon they undertook so many various and foolish Vows, Pilgrimages, Worshipping of Images, Masses, buying of Dirges, and Prayers, many beat themselves with rods, others entred [sic] into the Carthusian Order, others embraced other things, though most grievous and severe, all which were the works of afflicted and troubled Consciences, and that very thing which Christ here foretold.[5]

Luther goes on to refer to monastics as the pope's "shaven and hooded Disciples" and says that these "men have filled the world with Chappels and muttering of prayers, and whatsoever they mutter, that they think they pray, when the whole desire of the heart is against God" (25). Furthermore,

> These are they [i.e., the pope, bishops and clergy] who have hid the true *Sun* [i.e., Christ] from us, and have set up the Worship of Idols and vain shadows, instead of the Worship of God; whilest they have taught wretched men to merit and deserve God, by their shaving, hoods, bellowings, Organ-pipes, and noise, and with a thousand other most trifling trifles. (31–32)

Interpreting Luke 21:25–36, Luther says that the falling of stars predicted by the gospel writer refers to a baptized Christian becoming a priest or a

---

4. Ibid., 331.

5. Luther, *Signs of Christ's Coming*, 11–12. Hereafter cited parenthetically by page number.

monk, for "whoever becomes a Priest or Monk, with this opinion, that he thinks in so doing, he embraces *a saving kind of life*, he departs from the *Faith* of *Christ* to Infidelity." In short, priests and monks are true deniers of Christ and are without the hope of amendment "except God help by a miracle" (32).

Continuing in this vein is William Nicholls, Oxford University doctor and Anglican canon of Chichester Cathedral. In 1691 he published a response to the atheist Arthur Bury's *Naked Gospel* in which he acknowledged that "errours and Superstitions were every day crowding into the Church," as were "the Sacrifice of the Mass, Prayers for the Dead, Relics, Doctrine of Merits, Prayers in an unknown Tongue, Purgatory, Prohibition of Marriage in the Clergy, Monastic Life, Superstitions, Meats, Vests, [and] Tonsures." Despite these errors, writes Nicholls, Bury should still accept the Christian faith. Elsewhere, Myles Davies published an article in *Blackwood's Edinburgh Magazine* where he too speaks ill of monasticism. Davies was born into a Roman Catholic family and was educated for the Roman Catholic priesthood in Rome, where he was ordained in 1688. Yet, he later recanted his Roman Catholic faith and became an Anglican, publishing his recantation in 1705. In 1715 he began publishing his *Athenae Britannicae*, a history of critical writing in Oxford and Cambridge. In this text he refers, again derogatorily, to monasticism as "monkism." A similar use of "monkism" occurs in volume 64 of *Blackwood's Edinburgh Magazine* for 1848, in an article titled "Life and Times of George II," in which the House of the Stuarts is said to have "passed away—they mouldered from the sight of men; they have no more place or name on earth; they have been sunk in the mire of their monkism." Clearly, some Protestants have had harsh words regarding monasticism! But not all.

As demonstrated in the chapter on the Protestant Reformers below, Ulrich Zwingli easily criticizes the practice of monks and nuns. However, in the very same treatise in which he scathingly attacks the monastic lifestyle, he also allows for monasticism, or at least acknowledges some goodness in the institution itself. He believes that some of the original founders of religious orders were holy men who would have looked upon sixteenth-century Roman Catholic monasticism in dismay. He writes, "Were Francis, Dominic and the others here today they would undoubtedly say, 'You are out of your mind! What are you doing? Don't you know that you should have no other Teacher, Father or Leader than God? Why do you dedicate yourselves to us when our whole lives were attached to God alone?'" In Zwingli's mind, these men, whom he appears to respect as genuine Christians since

Reforming the Monastery

he does not call them the "anti-Christs," as he calls other Roman Catholics, would certainly not approve of the behavior of the sixteenth-century orders that bore their names. Though Zwingli says that unholy, covetous monks and nuns are "pigs in disguise," he confesses that there are some "godly member[s] of an order." These "honest consciences in the cowls who truly believe and follow the teaching of Christ" must do penance, however, for all the evil monastics inhabiting Reformation-era monasteries. That said, Zwingli does believe that monks and nuns should leave the cloister, yet if they "must," due to poverty and despair, they may remain in the cloister. However, Zwingli ultimately says that it is better if men and women do not become monks and nuns but instead "make themselves conform to the whole Christian community."[6] It is important to note, though, that Zwingli does leave a bit of room for someone to remain a monastic, which is a significant allowance coming from one who held such strong anti-monastic biases.

While the Reformation raged in Germany and many abandoned the monastic life due to the influence of the writings of Martin Luther and other reformers, there were some who continued to live a monastic life despite having adopted Protestant theology. In a letter addressed to the Benedictine abbot of Oldenstadt, Heino Gottschalk, Luther assures the abbot that true freedom is found in the monastery when one understands that one cannot earn his or her own salvation. Heino, the letter states, was experiencing a conflict of conscience because he felt unable to abandon the monastic life for fear of risking the salvation of his soul. Luther responds that if a monk or nun, like Heino, is moved by the Holy Spirit in his pursuit of virtue to be a monk, then he may remain in the monastery and may do so in the freedom of the Holy Spirit. Heino, taking this message to heart, remained a Protestant monk to the end of his life. Many other monasteries in Germany also converted to the Protestant faith while remaining true monasteries, though many of them adjusted their apostolates to become centers of education. For example, the Cistercian abbey of Loccum, founded originally in 1163 in Lower Saxony, became a "Protestant monastery" in 1593 and was greatly strengthened during the abbacy of Gerard Wolter Molanus. Once the monastery converted to Protestantism and adopted the Augsburg Confession (proof of its true Lutheran conversion), its monks were no longer required to take the vows of poverty, chastity, and obedience. Rather, the monastery community was now mostly composed of Lutheran

---

6. All quotations are from Pipkin, "Zwingli, the Laity and the Orders."

Introduction

clergymen, many of whom were married. Here and elsewhere, especially in Germany, many other monasteries that came over to the Reformation cause continued to live according the rules of the Cistercians, Augustinians, and Benedictines, or at least they lived according to adapted versions of these monastic rules. As one sermon from the Protestant monastery of Loccum states, it is a contradiction in terms to talk about a monk without a rule. Therefore, the author says that the Loccum abbey follows the Rule of Benedict along with the statutes of the Cistercian Order in such a way that the "Protestant religion is not revoked or changed." Elaborating further, Dorothea Wendebourg has written that "these communities followed strict rules in the tradition of the old orders, which included obedience toward the abbot/abbess or prior/prioress, celibacy, monastic hours, and a monastic habit. There were no vows."[7]

Within the Swiss Anabaptist Reformation tradition, there are several notable examples of monks adopting the Protestant faith while remaining for some time in the cloister or friary. For example, the Franciscan Peter Breit was placed on trial in Bern, Switzerland, in May 1527 for submitting himself to adult baptism, believing that faith must precede baptism. Though he ultimately recanted and continued to reject the theology of the magisterial reformers, Breit remained sympathetic to the Anabaptist position on baptism while remaining a Franciscan friar. Also, Anabaptist leader Nikolaus Guldin wrote a letter to "the sisters in the cloister" at Aarau. In this letter, Guldin appears to refer to the nuns not only as sisters in the religious sense but also as "sisters" in the Anabaptist faith, calling them "my beloved sisters in the Lord Jesus."[8] If so, the community can rightly be considered an Anabaptist monastic community.

Though many more examples of Anglicans favorable to monasticism will be given in chapter 2, two examples will suffice here. In England, despite the suppression of the monasteries by King Henry VIII beginning in the 1530s, the great playwright William Shakespeare presented the monastic life favorably, especially in his play *Measure for Measure*. In the very first act, Theseus, Duke of Athens, says to Hermia, who has just rejected her father's attempt to marry her to a man named Demetrius:

> Therefore, fair Hermia, question your desires,
> Know of your youth, examine well your blood,

---

7. Wendebourg, "Luther on Monasticism," 351.
8. Davis, *Anabaptism and Asceticism*, 113.

Reforming the Monastery

> Whether, if you yield not to your father's choice,
> You can endure the livery of a nun,
> For aye to be in shady cloister mewed,
> To live a barren sister all your life,
> Chanting faint hymns to the cold fruitless moon.
> Thrice blessèd they that master so their blood
> To undergo such maiden pilgrimage;
> But earthlier happy is the rose distilled
> Than that which, withering on the virgin thorn,
> Grows, lives, and dies in single blessedness. (1.1.67–78)

Here married life is said to be "earthlier happy" whereas the monastic life is truly "blessed." Though Shakespeare's own personal religious convictions are often debated, his corpus can be read as being generally sympathetic to the institution of monasticism. As well, it has been suggested by J. F. C. Harrison that the Shakers, a communitarian and pacifist group that grew out of the Quaker revival in England in 1747 under the leadership of Ann Lee, were "a kind of lay monasticism."[9] The community was dedicated to celibacy and to a common ownership of all goods. Members themselves were organized into orders or classes based on one's degree of commitment to the group. Those newest to the group comprised the novitiate order and were allowed to retain their own property and family life. In the next order, the junior level, one still owned her own property, but its use was dedicated to the larger Shaker community. In the highest order, the member signed over all goods to the community. Though not necessarily a clear advocation of monasticism as an institution, the Shakers appear to have been in favor of those aspects oftentimes seen as essential to the monastic life: personal poverty, celibacy, and communal living.

Jodocus van Lodenstein was a Dutch theologian of the seventeenth century who studied under the great Calvinist theologian, Gisbertus Voetius. Having lived a rather ascetical youth, as well as having immersed himself in the writings of the twelfth-century Cistercian abbot Bernard of Clairvaux and the fifteenth-century monk Thomas á Kempis, van Lodenstein, in 1659, made a particular bent toward mystical theology, which he describes as that which deals with "inexpressible things." Retreating to his monastic-like home, "The Park," van Lodenstein expressed an appreciation for monasticism. According to his biographer Carl Schroeder, moving

---

9. Harrison, *Second Coming*, 165.

into "The Park" "was certainly an attempt to create a cloistered, monastic setting. This side of van Lodenstein longed for and did approach the lifestyle characteristic of a religious order." Van Lodenstein himself wrote in his *Contemplation of Zion* (1674) that "the removal or throwing away of many things [in the Reformation], and what had followed that, had thrown out the good with the evil and also done great harm to the truth." One example of "the good" that had been thrown out were "the manifold orders and monasteries of monks and spirituals. . . . Alas, that men have stamped out the grand."[10] Another Calvinist who was not so understanding of monasticism was Jonathan Edwards. In his well-known *Religious Affections*, he writes that self-denial "consists in two things, viz., *first*, in a man's denying his worldly inclinations, and in forsaking and renouncing all worldly objects and enjoyments; and, *secondly*, in denying his natural self-exaltation, and renouncing his own dignity and glory and in being emptied of himself; so that he does freely and from his very heart, as it were renounce himself, and annihilate himself." Yet, he continues,

> Many anchorites and recluses have abandoned (though without any true mortification) the wealth and pleasures and common enjoyments of the world, who were far from renouncing their own dignity and righteousness. They never denied themselves for Christ, but only sold one lust to feed another; sold a beastly lust to pamper a devilish one; and so were never the better, but their latter end was worse than their beginning. They turned out one black devil to let in seven white ones that were worse than the first, though of a fairer countenance.[11]

Clearly Edwards was not as open to monasticism as his theological forefather, van Lodenstein.

Jumping ahead to the present, for the purpose of illustration, in 1999, George Carey, the Evangelical Archbishop of Canterbury, addressed the delegates at the Church of England's General Synod, taking an opportunity to promote the growth of monasticism in his own Protestant church tradition. Monasticism is a "witness to values which are so often scorned in our society," he said. As well, he confessed that the "archbishop is evangelical, but not narrowly so, and religious communities also transcend the pigeonholes that some wish to place them in. . . . [The] common assumption of many outside the church might well be that religious communities are out

---

10. Schroeder, *In Quest of Pentecost*, 83.
11. Edwards, *Religious Affections*, 241.

of touch and irrelevant. But my experience has shown that in the praying life of religious communities there is the greatest understanding of mission and unity." Though not explicitly Anglican communities, two examples of the kind of communities described by Archbishop Carey are the ecumenical monasteries of Taizé in France and Iona in Scotland.

The Taizé community was founded in 1940 by the Protestant Roger Louis Schütz-Marsauche, commonly known as Brother Roger (1915–2005). The son of a Swiss Protestant pastor and French Protestant mother, Roger studied Reformed theology in Strasbourg and Lausanne before moving to the small French town of Taizé in 1940, at the age of twenty-five. By 1944, Roger was living in simple poverty and obedience with a small community of men. On Easter Day 1949, the community numbered seven men who committed themselves to lifelong celibacy and life together in great simplicity. The Rule of Taizé, which now governs the community, was written by Roger in 1952–53. When discussing Taizé in his *Wellsprings of Christian Renewal*, Donald Bloesch, whose work will be treated in detail in chapter 4, writes that the community "seeks to instill new life into the churches of the Reformation." Though this is likely still the case, today there are approximately one hundred brothers who come from the Roman Catholic, Eastern Orthodox, and Protestant Christian traditions. The monastery is truly an ecumenical monastery as much as it is a Protestant monastery.

Another well-known ecumenical monastery is that of Iona, a small island in the Inner Hebrides of Scotland. The earliest monastic community to ever settle at Iona was that founded by Columba (also known as Columcille) in 563 and was still in existence up to the time of the dissolution of the monasteries by Henry VIII in the 1530s. At that time its buildings were destroyed and monastic life on the island ceased. The modern ecumenical monastery traces its origins to 1938, when George F. MacLeod, a Scottish Presbyterian minister, saw the lack of attention that the church paid to ministering to the physical and socials needs of its people. Resigning his parish, he gathered together a group of ministers and laypersons from various Protestant denominations to literally rebuild monastic life on Iona. Since that time, the community has maintained a small residential presence on the island with other members spread throughout the world. According to their website, the members meet throughout the year in local groups and four times yearly in "plenary gatherings, including a week on Iona." The community's rule of life is simple: daily prayer and Bible reading, mutual sharing and accountability of time and finances, regular meeting together and "action and reflection for justice, peace and the integrity of creation."

Introduction

Finally, there is the "new monasticism" of the North American Protestant church and the so-called secular monasticism found in England.[12] The September 2005 issue of *Christianity Today* featured on its cover a picture of Shane Claiborne and the words "The New Monasticism." Claiborne, along with several other graduates of Eastern University, is the founder of the Simple Way in the Kensington district of Philadelphia. The article highlighted the emergence of the new monastics, referring to them as an "intentional community" and as the "new friars."[13] The article states that the birth of the new monasticism can be dated to a conference held in June 2004 at which the participants drew up a voluntary rule. This rule, consisting of twelve distinctives, would be the guide for those communities who were voluntarily associating themselves with the new monastic movement. Since this time, these distinctives and their explication have been published as *School(s) for Conversion: Twelve Marks of a New Monasticism* by Cascade Books. This new monastic movement, made up of a diverse number of people and communities, describe themselves on their website as "a bunch of Jesus followers who have committed ourselves to a new way of life in community." One of the leaders of the new monastic movement, Jonathan Wilson-Hartgrove, author of *New Monasticism: What It Has to Say to Today's Church*, also lists the "twelve marks of a new monasticism" as the guiding principles for these new communities and identifies the June 2004 conference as a significant marker in the history of the movement. A more focused definition of new monasticism is found in an article by Robin Russell in *The United Methodist Reporter* titled "Intentional Community: New Monasticism Encourages Disciplined Life." Russell details how the new monastic movement is taking root in the United Methodist Church in North America. She writes that the new monasticism is characterized by individuals "living out their calling through disciplined and contemplative spiritual practices, participating in community life, and serving God and others."[14] Further, these new monastics "commit to follow a 'rule of life' . . . and they immerse themselves in community life and service."[15]

The secular monasticism of England is centered on the group "Monos: A Centre for the Study of Monastic Culture and Spirituality." The website

---

12. For an excellent introduction to the new monastic movement and important publications, see Carter, "New Monasticism."

13. Moll, "New Monasticism."

14. Russell, "Intentional Community," par. 7.

15. Ibid., par. 8.

describes their work as follows: "The Interest in the fruits of traditional monastic spirituality has blossomed in recent years. This blossoming has taken many forms; books, courses and websites have been written while some people attempt to live out those insights in communities, where they are and in what they can do in their daily lives. Again, this has taken many forms but generally come under the umbrella terms of 'New' 'Lay' or 'Secular' Monasticism. In the midst of this occurrence, The Monos Institute has been formed, in an attempt to offer a facility for the on-going dialogue between monastic spirituality, society, culture and Church. The Institute asks serious questions concerning the relationship between this New Monasticism, Church and society, both historically and contemporarily."[16] The Monos group sponsors regular seminars on secular monasticism and partners with traditional monastic communities (such as Douai Abbey) to explore monastic culture and spirituality. Unlike the new monasticism of the United States, the secular monastic movement in England seems more connected to traditional monasticism. For now, suffice it to say that both the new monastic movement and the secular monastic movement are highly supportive of diverse forms of monasticism, similar in spirit to van Lodenstein and Carey and, as we will see, others.

In a recent post to a *Christianity Today* blog called "The Monks Did It," theologian Chris Armstrong, just prior to venturing off to attend the annual Medieval Institute in Kalamazoo, Michigan, wonders why he is drawn to the medieval church. His answer: "Maybe it's the new monastics' fault." He elaborates by saying that the new monastics have afforded the Evangelical church of today an opportunity to engage in "some interesting meditations on the value for today's Christians of monastic disciplines." For Armstrong, as for me, this is a really good thing! Thus, with the rise of the new monasticism in the North American Evangelical church and secular monasticism in England, it is necessary to know what is "old" in order to move forward with the "new." In 1833, Oxford University professor Richard Froude wrote to John Henry Newman that "the present state of things in England makes an opening for reviving the monastic system." Seemingly original words at the time, yet monasticism is one of the most ancient and enduring institutions of the Christian church, reaching its zenith during the High Middle Ages. Although medieval monasteries were regularly suppressed during the Reformation and the magisterial Reformers rejected monastic vows in particular, the existence of monasticism has remained

---

16. See http://www.monos.org.uk/Monos-MonosInstitute.

Introduction

within the Reformation churches, both as an institution and in its theology. This volume is an examination of Protestant theologies of monasticism, examining the thought of select Protestant authors who have argued in depth for the existence of monasticism in the Reformation churches, beginning with Martin Luther and John Calvin and including John Henry Newman and the Tractarian movement, Karl Barth, Dietrich Bonhoeffer, Donald Bloesch, and others. This work is intended to supplement and move forward the discussion begun in other works on Protestant monasticism, such as François Biot's *Rise of Protestant Monasticism* and Donald Bloesch's *Centers of Christian Renewal* and *Wellsprings of Renewal*, both of which are now dated and were always somewhat incomplete.

Thus, in chapter 1, I will primarily discuss the monastic theology of the reformers Martin Luther and John Calvin, showing both their strong criticisms of monasticism while also highlighting their positive assessments of the monastic movement. While it is often categorically stated that Protestant theologians of the Reformation dismissed the presence of the monastic life in the church, this chapter will demonstrate that though Luther and Calvin did in fact reject a certain kind of monasticism, they did not reject all forms of monasticism. In chapter 2, I will distill the monastic theology of John Henry Newman, Oxford University professor and, in time, cardinal of the Roman Catholic Church, and his associates known as Tractarians or Anglo-Catholics. This nineteenth-century reintroduction of monasticism into the Anglican tradition firmly placed monasticism into the Protestant church in ways that were not previously known. Though the number of monasteries and monks and nuns in the Anglican Communion today continues to drop, the reasons provided by Newman and his colleagues for the presence of monasticism continue to remain persuasive. Karl Barth and Dietrich Bonhoeffer, twentieth-century European theologians, are the subject of chapter 3. Using his *Church Dogmatics* primarily, Barth's conception of the spiritual life and his comments on monasticism will show that Barth, who was influenced by Pietists like Tersteegen, saw great benefit in the presence of monasticism in the Protestant church. Bonhoeffer's own experiments in communal living will also reveal his debt to the institution of monasticism. Chapter 4 will investigate the thought of the late Donald Bloesch, contemporary American evangelical theologian, who for nearly fifty years argued for the practice of monasticism in the evangelical Christian tradition.

Before beginning, two definitions are in order. First, this text will understand "Protestant" in simple terms, as those Christian traditions that are not in communion with the Bishop of Rome (i.e., *not* Roman Catholic) and are not one of the geographical manifestations of the Eastern (now Western too) Orthodox Church. Though some Anglicans in the Anglo-Catholic tradition, for example, would not self-identify as Protestant, for the purposes of this book they will be labeled as Protestant, since they are neither in communion with the Bishop of Rome nor are they Eastern Orthodox. Second, "monasticism" will be understood as referring to those men and women who either live alone, in a solitary manner, or to a group of men or women who live together in community striving towards a common end and engaged in a shared apostolate. A rule, whether written or simply understood, is also a common feature of Christian monasticism.[17] So what, then, are Protestant theologies of the monastic life?

---

17. For further discussion on "monasticism," see Peters, "Monasticism."

ONE

The Protestant Reformers

It is generally concluded that the Protestant Reformers protested not against monastic life as such, but against the theological understanding of this kind of life in which free grace is replaced by works-righteousness. This conclusion is certainly borne out in the writings of Martin Luther, and it is this particular understanding of the monastic life, alongside other concerns, that motivates Luther's (at times) harsh rhetoric against the institution of monasticism. John Calvin, on the other hand, had a different set of concerns that motivated his writings against monasticism, as did other Reformers. This chapter will investigate the writings of Luther, Calvin, and other important Reformers regarding their views of monasticism. Though they oftentimes judged monasticism harshly, the Reformers, as will be seen, left the door slightly ajar for seeing the institution of monasticism in positive terms.

MARTIN LUTHER

Martin Luther was born on November 10, 1483, destined by his father to become a lawyer. He entered the University of Erfurt in 1501, graduating with his master's degree in 1505. Attempting to please his father, Luther enrolled in the school of law at Erfurt but very soon thereafter dropped out, subsequently entering the Augustinian friary at Erfurt in July, 1505. A very conscientious and introspective young man, Luther's time in the monastery proved difficult as he fretted about his salvation and ongoing sin. In later life, he described his time in the monastery as a time when he "lost hold of

Christ the Savior and comforter and made of him a stock-master and hangman over [his] poor soul."[1] As Luther strove to be the best monk that he could be, he continued to sense his failure as a monk and feared for his salvation. After receiving his doctorate in theology in 1512, Luther was tasked to lecture on the books of Psalms, Romans, and Galatians at the University of Wittenberg. It was during his course of studies on these books that he came to see that justification is by faith alone through grace and comes by way of faith in Jesus Christ. This insight put Luther at odds with the official teaching of the Roman Catholic Church, as did Luther's stance against the church's selling of indulgences. On January 3, 1521, Pope Leo X excommunicated Luther, finalizing Luther's break with the Roman Catholic Church. On June 13, 1525, Luther married the former Cistercian nun Katherine von Bora, finalizing his break with the institution of monasticism. There are two texts of Martin Luther's in particular where we are able to see his views clearly on the institution of monasticism: *The Freedom of a Christian* (written in October 1520) and *The Judgment of Martin Luther on Monastic Vows* (written in 1521 but published in February 1522).

The Freedom of a Christian was written in both German and Latin, with the German edition intended for the laity and the Latin edition intended for the more educated reader. In the German edition, Luther states that the purpose of the work is "to discern what a Christian person is and what freedom Christ has acquired and given this person."[2] For Luther, a "Christian person is a free sovereign, above all things, subject to no one." At the same time, a "Christian person is a dutiful servant in all things, subject to everyone" (70). These two contradictory positions, asserts Luther, are held in balance by the fact that one is relative to the soul and spiritual, while the other is related to the flesh and is physical. The Christian's freedom belongs to the inward, spiritual person, since nothing external can make a person free, because "freedom and righteousness . . . are not bodily or external" (71). What Luther is stating here is that there is a disconnect between that which is spiritual and that which is material. This is not some form of Greek dualism but is, instead, an insight of Luther into how we are as believers. For "What help is it to the soul if the body is not captive, fresh, and healthy, and eats and drinks, and lives as it wants? From the other perspective, what harm comes to the soul if the body is confined, sick, and

---

1. Kittelson, *Luther the Reformer*, 79.

2. Krey and Krey, *Luther's Spirituality*, 70. Hereafter cited parenthetically by page number.

weary, and hungers, thirsts, and suffers in the way it does not like?" This conclusion allows Luther to begin arguing that how one behaves outwardly, that is, their state of life, does not have a direct bearing on one's soul and, by extension, one's level of justification or holiness. For example, says Luther, "it does not help the soul at all if the body puts on holy clothing as the priests and clergy do, nor does it help to be in churches and sacred places." The only thing that can make the soul "alive, righteous, free and Christian" (71) is the gospel and the word of God preached by Christ.

This leads Luther to a discussion of what exactly constitutes the word of God: "It is nothing but the preaching of Christ in accordance with the gospel, spoken in such a way that you hear your God speaking to you. It shows how your whole life and work are nothing before God but must eternally perish with everything that is in you." In this way, Christians come to see their depravity and that they are bound for destruction. Yet, it is also the word of Christ that brings the Christian assurance that she can move beyond this state of destruction to a state of redemption. For this purpose "God places the dear Son, Jesus Christ, before you and allows you to be addressed by this living and comforting Word." The purpose of this revelation of the Son of God is so that each person will surrender himself or herself to the Word and trust in God alone for salvation. In this manner, "all your destruction will be overcome, and you will be righteous, genuine, satisfied, upright, and fulfill all the commandments and be free of all things" (72). True freedom, writes Luther, comes by way of one's full justification by faith in Jesus Christ. The implication of this theology, of course, is that good works no longer justify but are the result of one's justification. Works become those actions and dispositions that are for the purpose of practicing and strengthening the faith "because no other work can make a Christian." In short, Luther wants to make sure his readers understand that "faith alone without any works makes one righteous, free, and blessed" (73). Thus, "This is Christian freedom: faith alone, which brings about not that we might become idle or do evil but that we have need of no works to attain righteousness and blessedness" (75).

Now that Luther has laid the foundation for the spiritual and that which is relative to the soul, in the second part of *The Freedom of a Christian* he concerns himself with the outward person. Luther imagines, based on his previous arguments regarding the nature of faith, that someone could be tempted, like the so-called rich fool in the Gospel of Luke, to simply "relax, eat, drink, be merry" (12:19). That is, since faith alone is sufficient to make one righteous, why should one go about doing good works? Luther believes that the believer's perfection will occur only at "Judgment Day"; therefore, in this life, the "Christian person is a dutiful servant and subject to everyone." Again, though the Christian is free, she is also a servant, under obligation to do "all kinds of things." From the perspective of the soul, one is justified through faith and has everything necessary for salvation, even while one's faith and trust in God should continue to grow until they reach heaven. "However," Luther writes, "one still remains in this bodily life on earth and must rule one's own life and relate with people. Now works begin to play a role, and one must not be idle." Works are the result of faith and are not constituent parts of or necessary to faith. The good works that result from faith are manifested in the life of the believer by "fasting, waking, working, and every discipline in moderation" (81).

When the Christian attempts to do these good works as a manifestation of her inward justification, she "discovers a recalcitrant will that wants to serve the world and seek its own pleasure" (81). Faith is unable to tolerate this disobedient will, so it attempts to discipline it. Here Luther quotes from 1 Corinthians 9:27 ("I punish my body and enslave it") and Galatians 5:24 ("Those who belong to Christ... have crucified the flesh with its passions"), showing that this disciplining of the will takes a very physical, bodily form. In spite of the believer's need to discipline his body, these works must never be seen as causing one's righteousness, says Luther. Since the believer is already righteous by faith, these good works are the result of that faith, not necessary to instill or activate one's faith. Luther states, "Works should be done only with the idea that the body becomes obedient and purified of its evil passions" (81). Again, we see in Luther the close connection between works and the mortification of the body. Because the soul is purified, it longs to see the body purified also. In summary,

> Thus these two verses are true: Good and righteous works will never make a good and righteous person, but a good and righteous person does good and righteous works. Evil works never make an evil person, but an evil person does evil works. Therefore, the person must always be good and righteous beforehand, ahead of all good works, and good works follow and flow out of a righteous and good person. (83)

In the third section of *The Freedom of a Christian*, Luther turns from bodily good works to consider good works as being "useful and serving other people" (86). Having in mind the needs of others, says Luther, is evidence of the genuine Christian life. As slaves, Christians "become willing servants once again in order to help the neighbor" (87). This other-centeredness that flows out of one's faith is evidenced by love for one's neighbor and *not* by one's fixation on their own spiritual life. From this perspective, Luther commends monasticism, as long as it has the good of others in mind: "All the works of priests, monasteries, and religious foundations should be done in the same way too, that all do the work of their position in life or order for nothing else than the welfare of others." The priests, monks, and nuns should rule their bodies, for example, in such a way as to be an example for others to do the same. However, this is often not the case since "commands and laws of the pope, bishops, monasteries, foundations, rulers, and lords" (88) stipulate and insist that these good works done for the example and benefit of others are not the results of one's justification, but are necessary to be justified. It is necessary, then, that the believer judge rightly between the commands "of the blind and mad prelates and the right-minded ones" regarding his involvement in living the monastic life, since any work that is not oriented toward serving another is not a good, Christian work. "I worry," writes Luther, "that few foundation churches, monasteries, altars, masses, and testaments are Christian and, along with that, the special fasting and prayers to some of the saints. For I fear that in all of these works each person seeks only his or her own benefits, presuming thereby to do penance for his or her sins and be saved" (89).

Though Luther is not adamantly against monasticism per se in *The Freedom of a Christian*, he is concerned that many who practice it or may practice it will come to see it as salvific, as opposed to a fruit or good work of one's faith. Having been inwardly justified, the believer is expected, since she is a slave, to do good works, especially for the benefit of others. Yet, there are those in the Roman Catholic Church, says Luther, who would attempt to reverse the *ordo salutis* from "justification by faith leads to good works" to "good works lead to justification." This is *the* error of the late medieval Roman Catholic Church, according to Luther, and it leads him to believe that there are many called to be monks and nuns who do it only because some "evil" or "mad" prelate convinced them that they should do so for the sake of their salvation, rather than for the good of the world and their neighbor. Luther, however, has other reasons to question the validity of monasticism, especially the vows taken by those who choose to live this manner of life.

Reforming the Monastery

In 1521, a priest residing in a village near Wittenberg, Bartholomew Bernhardi, married with the consent of his parish. The Archbishop of Mainz and Magdeburg, Albert, demanded that Frederick of Saxony turn over the offending priest to the ecclesiastical authorities, but Frederick refused, instead referring the case to a commission of jurists. This led Philip Melanchthon, Luther's fellow reformer, to argue that it was both the Scriptures and the Christian tradition that allow priests to be married. Though "imprisoned" at Wartburg Castle at the time, Luther wrote *Theses on Vows* in 1521, arguing that vows of clerical celibacy contradict the fundamental principle of justification by faith and are therefore not binding on the individual. The following month, in a letter to George Spalatin, Luther noted the upcoming publication of a full work on monastic vows. This was further precipitated by the fact that many monks were leaving their monasteries, including the monks of Luther's own monastery in Wittenberg. When he returned from his "imprisonment" in Wartburg in spring 1522, the only person left in the monastery was the prior, Conrad Helt. Nearly thirty monks had left the monastery the previous November. As long as these men were leaving the monastery out of conviction from God and with a good conscience, Luther was supportive. However, he expected that many of these monks were leaving instead to avoid the discipline of the monastery and because they could not live up to the vows that they made before God. Thus, *The Judgment of Martin Luther on Monastic Vows* was intended to serve as a guide for those who had left the monastic enclosure or were thinking about doing so. After a delay, the book was published in February 1522 with a revised edition published in June 1522. Both the original text and the revised text were translated into German in the same year.

The preface to *On Monastic Vows* was a letter that Luther wrote to his father on November 21, 1521. In this letter, Luther explains to his father his need to enter into the monastic life and how now, in hindsight, he sees the folly in his decision. He first explains to his father that he had primarily entered the monastery due to "the terror and the agony of sudden death," that is, when he had feared for his life during a lightning storm near Stotternheim in 1505.[3] He then admits to his father that his monastic vows were "not worth a fig" since they had been taken in such a way as to violate God's commandment of honoring one's father and mother: "It was a wicked vow, and proved that it was not of God not only because it was a sin against your authority, but because it was not absolutely free and voluntary" (332) due to

---

3. Luther, *Luther's Works*, 48:332. Hereafter cited parenthetically by page number.

Luther's fear following the lightning storm. Luther, however, is thankful for the experience of being a monk living under vows, so that when he attacks those who perpetuate such errors he can oppose them from firsthand experience as opposed to writing and speaking about something with which he has no experience. In Luther's estimation, monastic vows are a sign of human presumption and are the result of the "mad and silly papists" (333) exalting the virtue of continence and virginity to be the highest states of the spiritual life. In Luther's opinion, the Scriptures approve virginity, but they do not praise it as a higher state than the married life. Thus, the Roman Catholic hierarchy is in gross error when they make virginity out to be a higher, more holy form of life than the married estate.

Luther continues by asking his father whether he seeks to remove him now from the monastery, just as he had wished to do in 1505. The younger Luther asks, "What difference does it make whether I retain or lay aside the cowl and tonsure? Do [they] make the monk?" (334–35). Martin Luther believes that the most important development in his life in his years as a monk is that he now realizes that the cowl and tonsure do not make the monk; rather, since God makes the monk, Luther's conscience is free. He concludes that "I am still a monk and yet not a monk" (335). It appears that Luther, at this point, is willing to view himself as a monk, not because he is under vows, but because he is choosing, in the freedom of Christ, to be a monk. Yet he also acknowledges that he is no longer a monk, as God "has taken [him] out of the monastery" (335) and placed him in his true service. This makes God Luther's "bishop, abbot, prior, lord, father, and teacher" (336), as opposed to any human claiming this right. Luther concludes by extolling his freedom from papal tyranny, set free in service to God, no longer bound by vows.

In *On Monastic Vows* itself, Luther makes the broad argument that since there are scriptures that insist on vow-keeping, the main issue at stake in the question of monastic vows is whether they are, in fact, vows at all. He describes the ways in which one can distinguish between true and false vows. The argument is laid out in five steps: 1) God's Word does not command monastic vows; 2) monastic vows are in conflict with faith; 3) the fact that monastic vows are compulsory and perpetual violates the freedom of a Christian; 4) monastic vows violate the Ten Commandments; and 5) monastic vows are contrary to common sense. The work concludes with a discussion of the true nature of poverty, chastity, and obedience, as well as with an exposition of 1 Timothy 5.

Reforming the Monastery

In the first section of *On Monastic Vows*, Luther argues that monastic vows are against God's word. He does this in three ways: 1) monastic vows are simply equivalent to baptismal vows; 2) scriptural commandments apply to all Christians since God makes no distinction between counsels and precepts like the Roman Catholic Church; and 3) virginity and celibacy are commandments given to all Christians inasmuch as individual believers are led to live virginal, celibate lives. "There is no doubt that the monastic vow is in itself a most dangerous thing because it is without the authority and example of Scripture," writes Luther.[4] In contrast to monastic vows, the scriptures stipulate that all believers are to be imitators of God and the Scriptures never permit the taking of vows, the forming of monastic orders, or the following of rules. Luther strongly states that the "Scriptures clearly compel us to condemn whatever is only a matter of rules, statutes, orders, schools of thought, and, in addition, whatever falls short of, is contrary to, or goes beyond Christ, even if these things had been handed over by angels from heaven or confirmed by mighty miracles" (254). Because they are unscriptural, therefore, no one is free to take monastic vows. Furthermore, monastic vows, says Luther, are none other than the very baptismal vows taken by all believers: "When a [monk] takes his vow he vows nothing more than that which he already vowed at the start in his baptism, and that is the gospel" (255). Instead of being built upon the common baptism of all believers, monastic vows imply that one can progress further along spiritually than even Jesus Christ himself: "Whatever is commanded which is contrary to or beyond Christ is condemned, whether a man takes it upon himself or whether he is following the example and teaching of the saints" (254). Anyone who has taken vows, then, must not fulfill them and anyone who has not taken vows is not at liberty to do so.

Next Luther lays out the two basic ideas of those who take vows. First, returning to the issue of how those under monastic vows elevate their spiritual life above that of other Christians, Luther explains that historically, though wrongly, the gospel has been divided into precepts and counsels. Those in monastic vows, supposedly, follow the counsels rather than the precepts, which are intended for "ordinary men." Luther believes that this misses the point of the gospel, which "is simply the promises of God declaring the benefits offered to man" (256), summed up especially in the Sermon on the Mount in Matthew 5–7. For Luther, there is only one gospel and it is binding on all Christians, regardless of one's state in life. The

---

4. Luther, *Luther's Works*, 44:252. Hereafter cited parenthetically by page number.

commandments in the Sermon on the Mount are exactly that—"necessary commandments" (258) that are "without a shadow of doubt, obligatory precepts taught by Christ" (259). Second, regarding the particular issue of virginity, which the Roman Church termed a counsel, Luther says, "Christ did not counsel it, but rather discouraged it. . . . He neither invites anyone to take up celibacy, nor calls men to it. He simply refers to it" (261). Neither did the Apostle Paul advise anyone to take up the life of virginity: "Paul neither persuades nor dissuades; he leaves the matter open" (262). This leads Luther to conclude that

> If celibacy is an evangelical counsel, what is the sense of your making a vow that goes beyond the gospel and makes a rigid commandment out of a counsel? For now you live not according to the gospel but beyond it. In holding this you even live contrary to the gospel and no longer have a counsel. If you obey the gospel, you ought to regard celibacy as a matter of free choice: if you do not hold it as a matter of free choice, you are not obeying the gospel. It is quite impossible to make an evangelical counsel into a precept, and it is equally impossible for your vow to be a counsel. A vow of chastity, therefore, is diametrically opposed to the gospel. (262)

When virginity is elevated to a higher state than that of the married life, as the Roman Catholic Church believed, this divides the Christian life into two states: perfection and imperfection. The monks and nuns, of course, are the perfect, whereas all others are viewed as imperfect. Luther sees that the Bible speaks clearly against the sin of lust, but he does not see it teaching the superiority of virginity over married life. Like the Apostle Paul in 1 Corinthians, Luther does confess that the unmarried are more effective servants of God. Yet, God does not praise the unmarried individuals simply *because* they are unmarried, but because they remain unmarried for the sake of the kingdom of heaven. Their end is not their own virginity as something to be praised, but the establishment of the kingdom of God. Luther concludes that the "man who most effectively serves the kingdom by preaching the gospel and propagating the faith among the people is one who is unmarried, who is free of family responsibilities and who lives a celibate life" (264). In short, monastic vows are against the word of God because they deny the baptismal vows taken by all Christians, they wrongly divide the biblical commandments into counsels and precepts, and they elevate virginity to a place where it creates two classes of believers, the perfect and the imperfect. For all of these reasons monastic vows are wrong, but there are others reasons for this to be true as well.

Luther next turns his attention to the fact that monastic vows, he believes, are against the Christian faith. This is important to Luther because, according to Romans 14:23, everything that is not of faith is sin; therefore, if monastic vows are against faith then they are sinful. Luther first argues that they are not of faith because they are permanent vows, that is, lifelong and compulsory. Vows based on faith, on the other hand, would allow someone "to keep them at one time or to renounce them at another" (273). Furthermore, returning to a theme from *The Freedom of a Christian*, Luther says that good works are the fruit of faith, thus they "do not really pertain to the remission of sins and a serene conscience, but are the fruits of a forgiveness already granted and still present." Works done before faith with the intention that they are salvific are sins, whereas the works done as a result of faith "are the fruits of a man who is already justified" and are motivated by faith and love (279). In Luther's estimation, it is "unchallengeable" that you can expect works to assist in the remission of sins. Thus, monastic vows taken with the assumption that they will aid in your justification are, in fact, sins. Luther returns to the believer's baptismal vows, stating that they are the only true vows born of faith. Monastic vows, which undermine the baptismal vows of all Christians, were thought of erroneously by the late medieval church to be a kind of second grace over and above baptismal vows. Speaking to this, Luther writes that "they think the grace of baptism has become worthless, and that now the shipwreck must be avoided by the 'second plan of penance' [i.e., the taking of monastic vows]" (280–81).

Switching gears, Luther now quotes 1 Timothy 4:1–3, saying that "on this text alone . . . I am bold enough to declare that all monks be absolved from their vows, and I pronounce with confidence that their vows are unacceptable and worthless in the sight of God" (282).[5] Refuting the notion that these passages referred historically to two particular groups of heretics, Luther concludes that they must refer "to the celibates among us—our pope, priests, monks and nuns" (284). Wondering aloud why this biblical passage has not caused all monks, nuns and priests to abandon their vows, Luther concludes that perhaps it is because they, like himself up to that

---

5. 1 Timothy 4:1–3: "Now the Spirit expressly says that in later times some will depart from the faith by devoting themselves to deceitful spirits and teachings of demons, through the insincerity of liars whose consciences are seared, who forbid marriage and require abstinence from foods that God created to be received with thanksgiving by those who believe and know the truth" (ESV).

time, imagine that they have entered into these vows voluntarily and are therefore not trusting in the vows as a source of salvation. Luther concludes that such thinking is wrong since he now knows, from 1 Timothy 4:1–3, that monastic vows are demonic and therefore *must* be rejected. To not do so, he thinks, proves the Apostle Paul's very point in the 1 Timothy passage. Yet, the monks and nuns go so far to show that their manner of life is godly that they "sell and exchange their good works, their merits, and their brotherhoods to others" (285). According to Luther, this makes them worse than all heathens. The particular way, in fact, that they are heathen is that they play the role of Christ. By Luther's time, it had become a somewhat common practice for individuals, on their deathbeds, to become a monk or nun. This, they believed, gave them the best chance of being saved. Luther sees this as a complete denial of the salvific work of Christ, since it places faith in the institution of monasticism and *not* the shed blood of Jesus Christ. In one sense, writes Luther, though the "papist monks" never refer to themselves by the word *Christ*, "nevertheless, they all say, 'I am Christ'; they abstain from using the name, but arrogate to themselves the office, the work and the person" (287). They teach others to trust in the merits of monasticism as opposed to trusting in the merits of Christ. Sparing no monk or nun, Luther sees this as abominable, referring to monks as apostates from the faith, Christ-deniers, and those who forsake the gospel and return to the rigorous moral demands of the Old Testament law. Succinctly put, they "return to one's heathen vomit" (288). Because of this heresy, all monastics should forsake their monastic vows.

Given this strong language and argumentation by Luther against monasticism, it would seem that he is absolutely against anyone becoming a monk or nun. Yet, he now moves into a discussion of "the holy and pious monks" who are much like Bernard of Clairvaux, the twelfth-century Cistercian abbot and theologian.[6] Luther states that Bernard and others like him understood that they were justified by faith alone and were not trusting in their good works for salvation. In Bernard's case, writes Luther, the abbot of Clairvaux did realize the futility of his monastic life. Turning to Bernard's twentieth sermon on the Song of Songs, Luther quotes, "I have lost my time because I have wasted my life. But one thing gives me solace. A

---

6. The Cistercians were founded in France in 1098 by Robert of Molesme as a reaction against the exaggerated Benedictine monasticism typical of the time. The intent of the Cistercian movement was to observe the Rule of Benedict with fidelity and to return to the simplicity of earlier monasticism. The movement spread rapidly and grew numerically large. The Cistercians still exist today.

broken and contrite heart thou dost not despise" (290). The context, however, of this quotation from Bernard is that one who lives their life without loving Jesus or fearing God is unworthy and ungrateful of God's grace and God's salvation. Bernard would seem to not be saying, "My monastic life has been pointless," but rather, "Even though I have lived as a monastic, I have not loved and feared God like I should." Bernard quotes King David from Psalm 51, David's psalm of repentance for his adultery with Bathsheba and murder of Uriah. Like David who is asking that God forgive him for his sin *despite* being God's anointed king and prophet, Bernard is asking for God's grace *despite* being a Cistercian monk and abbot. Luther seems to have missed the point that Bernard was making. Despite this, Luther's point here is to show that though there have been monks and nuns justified by faith who remained monks and nuns, that is no reason to make monastic vows binding on anyone. Following this line of thinking (i.e., that monastic life is superior to non-monastic life and therefore people should vow themselves to it), writes Luther, would mean that some people should take martyrs vows since martyrs are also approved of by God. Why not take vows that obligate one to suffer by fire, sword, cold, wild beasts and the cross since these actions could also be construed to be salvific? The answer: "These godless people not only want the monastic life to be regarded as a way of life in which a man may lead the good life, but rather as the way of life through which a man leads the good life—or, still better, the way of life which is good in itself" (291).

From these arguments Luther concludes that monastic vows "cannot be taught as being not more than and nothing other than faith" (292). They are ungodly, erroneous and even "satanic." Therefore, everyone under monastic vows must revoke them and give them up in confidence that they will be justified by faith and not by the good works of vows. In Luther's estimation, one can only teach the value of vows if vows are the means to an end—in this case, the means to justification. For why else, asks Luther, would anyone be interested in taking the vows unless they believed that the vows saved them? Thus, "Monastic vows and works, then, cannot be seriously taught and learned without those who teach them and those who learn them becoming apostates from Christ and falling from faith" (292–93). The Apostle Paul and Bernard of Clairvaux support this conclusion, though Luther misunderstood Bernard's words. Justification is by faith, thus one must trust in faith and not in vows.

Luther now turns his attention to the third step of his argument: monastic vows are against evangelical freedom since they resist the fruit of faith and the word of God. Luther says that since vows are not necessary for justification, they can be laid aside, for one would never lay aside necessary vows. Since monastic vows are not necessary then they must be able to be laid aside, therefore monastic vows *as* vows must, by definition, be "a matter of free choice and can be laid aside" (297). The core, then, of a monastic vow runs something like this, writes Luther: "I vow to thee this kind of life, which by its very nature is not necessary to attain righteousness, neither can it ever become a matter of necessity" (297). This embracing of Christian freedom does not mean that the biblical commandments do not need to be observed. Though the flesh is not justified by works of the law, says the Apostle Paul (see Rom 3:20), Matthew states that works are necessary (see Matt 19:17) and Peter requires a Christian to be virtuous (see 2 Pet 1:5). Laying aside a vow does mean laying aside good works since the freedom of the gospel cannot dispense with the commandments of God. Yet, what exactly is Christian freedom? Luther defines Christian (or evangelical) freedom as "a freedom of conscience which liberates the conscience from works" (298). This does not mean that the Christian does no works, but it does mean that a Christian puts no justifying power in those works. The conscience puts no trust in a person's works, but trusts fully in the works of Christ alone, for a believer is justified only by his works. Good works should be done freely and for no reward, especially as they are of benefit to our neighbor. This makes good works no longer works of the law (such as the Ten Commandments), but makes them works of Christ, "working in us through faith and living in us in everything we do. For that reason these works can no more be omitted than can faith itself, nor are they less necessary than faith" (301).

Continuing with this distinction that some vows are works of the law and others are works of Christ, Luther says that we undertake in our own effort vows that are works of the law; therefore, these vows should be given up and condemned as distractions that draw our consciences away from Jesus Christ. At other times, "vows are made through Christ working in us in the spirit of freedom, provided that they are taken and kept voluntarily, when neither satisfaction for sins is claimed by them, nor righteousness and salvation sought through them" (303). Christians are free to observe all the laws, rites, and customs made by humans as long as they are not contrary to the laws of God and are not trusted in for salvation. Thus, Christian freedom is freedom indeed, as long as it is not viewed as salvific. And this brings Luther to reach a conclusion regarding monasticism that is much more positive than anything said up to this point. Thus, it is worth quoting in full:

> If you vow to take up the religious life, and if you live with men of like mind, with a clear conscience that in monasticism you seek nothing to your advantage in your relationship with God, but because either your situation has brought you to embrace this kind of life, or it appeared to be the best way of life for you, without your thinking thereby that you are better than he who takes a wife or takes up farming, then in that case you are neither wrong to take vows nor wrong to live in this way, insofar as the propriety of the vow is concerned. But if love should demand that the vow be broken and you were to hold fast to your vow, you would be sinning, as we shall explain. (304)

Here we see Luther allowing for the institution of monasticism, as long as it is entered into with a clear conscience and God's leading. Though the monastic life was often taught historically to be the highest form of religious life, this form of monasticism described by Luther is not superior to other forms of life. It is equal to the married estate and any other Christian vocation. In light of this, it appears that Luther's vitriol up to this point in *On Monastic Vows* may have been motivated by the fact that he disliked the Roman Catholic Church more than by his dislike or disgust with the monastic life per se.

He continues by firmly establishing that certain kinds of lifestyles, virginity for example, are allowable, as long as the one engaged in the lifestyle does not view herself as superior to others. Luther acknowledges that virginity is "no light matter" (307), but if a virgin makes herself out to be superior to a married woman, then she is no longer a true virgin of God. The motivation to remain a virgin should be for Christian simplicity, so that the virgin can glory in Christ more easily than she who is married. This is consistent with Luther's interpretation of the Pauline admonition that "he who takes a virgin does well, but he who does not does better" (1 Cor. 7:38). To buttress his argument, Luther shows that the earliest church did not always view the virginal, monastic life as superior to the married life. Using examples from *The Lives of the Fathers* (*Vitae Patrum*), Luther says that even an "Alexandrian tanner was regarded as equal, indeed, superior to Anthony," the great Egyptian solitary immortalized by Athanasius in *The

Life of Anthony. *The Lives of the Fathers* reads, "Once when blessed Antony was praying in his cell he heard a voice saying, 'Antony you are not yet equal to the leather worker in Alexandria.' When he heard this, the old man got up next morning and taking his staff hastened off to Alexandria where he sought out the leather worker, who was absolutely astonished to be visited by such a great man."[7] As well, two married women and a former thief were said to be "equal to Paphnutius, an abbot of Thebes" (308). Concerning the former thief, *The Lives of the Fathers* says,

> After living a disciplined life for a long time, Paphnutius asked God to show him whether there was anyone else among the holy people living an upright life who compared to him. An angel appeared to him and said, "There is a flautist in this region like you." He hastily sought him out to find out how he lived and acquaint himself with everything he had done. "The truth is," the flautist said, "that I am a sinner, a drunkard and a fornicator. It is not long since I stopped being a thief."

Intent on knowing what this flautist and former thief has done to merit the angel's appellation that he is a holy as Paphnutius, the abbot pressed him to recall something good that he had done. In response, the former thief recalled a time when he had helped a woman who was wandering in the desert. The distraught woman explained that her husband was in prison for tax evasion and that her sons were taken from her. She is merely resigned to have the man take her as his servant. Instead, the former thief "took pity on her . . . and took her back to [his] cave, gave her three hundred gold pieces and took her back to the city where her husband and children were freed from all disgrace and shame." Paphnutius admits that he has never done something like that, so he invites the former thief to return to the desert with him to live the "disciplined life." At once, the flautist "threw away the flute he had in his hands and exchanged the music of lyric poetry for a melody of the spirit."[8] In Luther's estimation, therefore, he has demonstrated that there is an equality of holiness among both the non-celibate, non-monastics and those dedicated to the virginal, monastic life. This equality is born out of the fact that everyone's faith is the "same faith in Christ common to us all" (308).

---

7. Bk. 7, ch. 15. The full text of the *Vitae Patrum* is available online; see http://www.vitae-patrum.org.uk/page102.html.

8. Bk. 8, ch. 58.

Thus, since the same degree of holiness is available to everyone, regardless of whether they take a vow or not, then vows are unnecessary, even ungodly. And, again, vows are against evangelical freedom since they bind the Christian to a kind of unscriptural precept, whereas the Scriptures teach that there is freedom on such matters as food, clothing, places and the like. Reiterating what he has already established, Luther returns to the fact that the institution of monasticism, as it was then practiced, has made vows obligatory and therefore sinful when broken. Whereas sixteenth-century monasticism had made it sinful, God had made it life-giving: "You may take and keep all the vows you like, as long as you do no violence to the freedom commanded by God. You have no right at all either to take away that freedom or to set up sin where God has not willed sin to be" (311). The only solution, repeats Luther, is to conclude that vows are not permanent and are able to be retracted given one's life situation.

Luther now transitions to the fourth of five steps in *On Monastic Vows*—that monastic vows violate the commandments. Given that monastic vows are contrary to the Christian faith and to evangelical freedom, as well as against Scripture, Luther immediately concludes that monastic vows "cannot be anything else but contrary to all divine commandments when they are contrary to the One from whom and through whom and in whom all things exist" (317). For Luther, monastic vows are against the First Table, that is, against the first three of the Ten Commandments. The first commandment commands faith, the second commands praise and confession of the name of God, and the third commands the work of God in us. Monastic vows, which teach works, make "faith devoid of content" (318) and thereby they are against the first commandment. They transgress the second commandment when they cast aside the name "Christian" and adopt the name Benedictines, Dominicans, Franciscans or Augustinians. They no longer believe that they are saved by the name of "Christ" but think that they are saved "because they bear the name of their [monastic] order" (318). They transgress the third commandment when they are happier to have served the statutes of their order and followed the example of their founder than by serving Jesus Christ through the promises made in their baptismal vows. Monk and nuns seek to attain heaven by means of their own works as opposed to the works of God in Christ. Just as it is impossible for someone trusting in Christ to believe that their own works save them, it is impossible for the person who relies on "works and vows not to seek salvation in his own name" (320).

This leads Luther into a particularly acute anti-monastic rant. First, "the monastic institution is a seditious movement directed against Christ." Second, "monasticism encourages divisions among the people of Christ." Third, "its teaching is contrary to faith and causes men to have faith in their own works and to hold them in esteem." Fourth, any monk or nun who is a monk or nun that does not transgress the three aforementioned critiques "is a miracle of divine power, not a general rule for life" (321). Fifth, monastics think they are superior in holiness to all other Christians. In fact, Luther dares the monks and nuns to proclaim that "it is far better to be a Christian than a monk" (322). If they were to do this, very few monastics would remain in their cloisters. They only remain encloistered because they have adopted the false position that "monkery," to use Luther's word, is superior to all other forms of Christian life. Lastly, like the useless musical instruments mentioned by the Apostle Paul in 1 Corinthians 4:7, monks and nuns simply make noise. The praying of monastics is equivalent to a lecturer mounting the platform only to speak in an unintelligible language.

Monastic vows are also against the Second Table of the commandments, which can be summed up, writes Luther, "under two headings: obedience to parents and love of neighbor" (326). Luther writes that after faith there is nothing greater than the love of parents. Turning to 1 Timothy 5:4, Luther notes that even those who are widowed, if they have their own house or living parents, are not allowed to take a vow of celibacy and remain a widow.[9] This allows Luther to return to the nature of vows, which must be conditional, unless, he adds, these vows are vows of obedience to parents and love of neighbor: "Let the man be anathema who has taken a vow in conflict with his responsibility toward his parents and toward his neighbor" (326). This goes against monastic vows, believes Luther, since monasticism teaches that it is not possible to obey parents or care for others, due to the fact that a monk is "dead to the world, dedicated to God, and must do so much in the monastery that parents, neighbors, indeed, the whole world, can suffer distress, collapse, and perish" (327). That the institution of monasticism would allow children to forsake parents and neglect others is so abominable to Luther that he himself admits that this "is where [his] indignation is sorest" (327). Therefore, on this account alone, he wants "the whole idea of the monastery rooted out, wiped out, and abolished, as

---

9. Behind Luther's understanding of this passage is the long-standing interpretation of the text as teaching that in the earliest church there was a tradition that taught that these widows were a vowed order in the church. Just as overseers, priests, and deacons were unique offices in the church, so were widows, according to church tradition.

indeed it ought to be" (328). Like Sodom and Gomorrah were destroyed by fire and brimstone, so should the institution of monasticism!

In their defense, monks and nuns, writes Luther, offer several reasons for their "impiety": 1) since "obedience is better than sacrifice" (1 Sam 15:22), then serving neighbors can only be done with the monastic superior's permission; 2) spiritual fathers take precedence over natural fathers, therefore obedience to the former take precedence; and 3) love is evidenced in the monastery between the brothers as well as it is outside the monastery. In response to the first excuse, Luther says that 1 Samuel 15:22 applies to divine commands, not human commands and consequently this verse is actually an attack on monasticism. God does not find one's sacrifice of entering monastic life acceptable; instead, he rewards Christian obedience to all his commandments. In response to the second excuse, Luther says that a true spiritual father would not command anything contrary to love of parents and neighbor. Therefore, these so-called spiritual fathers are spiritual only in the sense that they "give heed to the spirits of error" (1 Tim. 4:1). Since they are not truly spiritual, one does not need to listen to them over one's natural father. In reality, a mother or a father has every right to remove a son or daughter from the monastery, no matter how many vows the child has taken. Addressing the final excuse, Luther insists that monks do not love rightly since they only love one another, whereas true Christian love "is free" and "directed to no person in particular" (333). The love of the monastery is a self-serving love, not an others-centered love as expected by God and commanded in the scriptures.

Luther then turns to the final step in his exposition against monastic vows: that monasticism is against common sense and reason. Beginning with reason, Luther says that it is wrong when it employs affirmative statements but when "it asserts negative statements its judgement is right" (336). That is, reason is unable to comprehend who God is but it is able to say what he is not. Reason is unable to see all that is right in God's eyes but it does know that certain moral actions are wrong, such as adultery, murder and disobedience. Is it possible then, asks Luther, to determine if the institution of monasticism is against reason? Yes, concludes Luther.

If it can be proven that there is one instance when a vow can be set aside then, believes Luther, all vows can be set aside. Suppose, he writes, that one makes a vow to go on a pilgrimage but is prevented from making the pilgrimage due to death, insufficient funds, illness, or incarceration. In this case, the vow is set aside. In the same way, if a person takes a vow of celibacy thereafter realizing that he is not able to keep the vow, then he is free to marry. Just like the vow to go on pilgrimage, the vow of celibacy can be laid aside. Luther includes examples from monastic texts where the austerity of monastic discipline is laid aside due to a monk or nun's inability to follow the letter of the rule. For example, in Augustine of Hippo's *Rule*, he writes that those who become monks but are not used to such extreme mortifications may receive "concessions" from the superior regarding their bedding, food, and clothing. Sick monks are also allowed dietary variation from the rule.[10] Further, Bernard of Clairvaux, in his *Precept and Dispensation*, says that every part of the monastic rule is in the hands of the superior, who is able to grant dispensations as she sees fit, whether for good or ill.[11] Ultimately then, writes Luther, the pope has "full authority to make or change all of the rules, and to grant dispensation" (344). Thus, monastic vows are not made to God but rather to one's father or mother superior. Reasonably, it can be concluded that if the vows can be laid aside for such pragmatic reasons, then it is clear that monastic vows are unreasonable, including celibacy. If other monastic vows are laid aside when convenient, then why not the most indispensable of all the vows—celibacy?

Luther admits that there is a strong tradition in the Christian church that asserts that once someone has lost her virginity it cannot be restored. Yet, Luther also acknowledges that there is also a tradition which says otherwise, whether through miraculous means or in some other manner. That the church has prized virginity so highly means that the institution of monasticism sees the vow of celibacy as binding. This leads Luther to conclude that vows are not kept because they are precepts, something that the church historically argued, but rather they are kept depending on their "importance or [their] insignificance, in the worth or the worthlessness" (347). Monks and nuns keep the vow of virginity because it is a "great thing," but they do not keep the other vows that they take with such stringency. In fact, the other vows can be dispensed with as necessary or on a whim "because they are unimportant matters" (347). Vows are kept then not because they lie in God's will but in the will of the one taking the vow, or at least in the will of the superior of the one taking the vow. This, without doubt, says Luther, greatly displeases God, who does not command the work but expects obedience in the work.

---

10. See Lawless, *Augustine of Hippo and His Monastic Rule*, 84–87.
11. See Bernard of Clairvaux, *Treatises I*.

Reforming the Monastery

John Calvin

John Calvin was born in 1509. In 1520 or 1521, he entered the Collège de la Marche for the primary purpose of learning to read and speak Latin well enough to proceed to the arts faculty at university, a prerequisite for studying theology. Within a year, however, Calvin was judged capable of starting the arts course, therefore he moved from La Marche to the Collège de Montaigu. This college, interestingly for the present study, was very "monastic" in its orientation. Jean Standonck had reformed the college forty years prior to Calvin's arrival. His goal, in imitation of the older religious orders, was to make Montaigu into a kind of educational monastery. The students recited the daily offices of prayer, the great feasts of the church calendar were celebrated, the student's moral life was strictly controlled, there was regular participation in public confession of sins, and a weekly examination into the student's behavior was conducted. Further, a kind of perpetual fast was kept, given that the food was minimal and of poor quality.[12] Perhaps it was here that Calvin got a taste of what the monastic life was like which he would later denounce, though not completely reject. At the age of fourteen, he began theology studies at the University of Paris, taking his MA. Perhaps as early as 1525/6, he moved to Orléans to study law and then transferred to Bourges to continue his studies in law. He returned to Orléans in October 1530, taking his *licentiate* in law in early 1531. Sometime between 1528 and 1530, Calvin underwent a conversion to Protestantism. Due to the persecutions of Protestants by Roman Catholics, Calvin left Paris in 1533, spending the next three years traveling throughout France, Italy, and Switzerland. In July 1536, Calvin arrived in Geneva on his way to Strasbourg when William Farel, another French reformer, convinced him to stay. When Geneva refused to reform itself along Calvin's lines, he and Farel left the city. He spent the next three years, from 1538 to 1541, in Strasbourg, returning to Geneva in 1541, where he was then able to institute all of his proposed reforms. Calvin remained in Geneva for the rest of his life, dying there in 1564.

Calvin's *Institutes of the Christian Religion* went through several editions in both French and Latin. The definitive edition is the Latin version of 1559. This work is broken down into four parts: the first is dedicated to God the Father; the second discusses God the Son; the third concerns itself with God the Holy Spirit under the title "The Way in which we Receive the Grace of Christ: What Benefits Come to us from It, and What

---

12. Parker, *John Calvin*, 4–7.

Effects Follow;" and the fourth part deals with the church. In the thirteenth chapter of the fourth book, Calvin takes up the topic of vows, particularly monastic vows. Like Martin Luther, Calvin is strongly against vows, yet unlike Luther, Calvin does not necessarily rail against individual monks, but in general condemns the institution of monasticism itself: "Let my readers accordingly remember that I have spoken rather of monasticism than of monks, and noted not those faults which inhere in the life of a few, but those which cannot be separated from the order of living itself."[13] Matthew Boulton summarizes well Calvin's overall approach to monasticism:

> Calvin grounds his quarrel with monasticism—in an endorsement of monasticism. That is, his argument hinges on a contrast between contemporary and ancient forms of monastic life. . . . For Calvin, monastics are mistaken only insofar as they make elite, difficult, and rare what should be ordinary, accessible, and common in Christian communities: namely, whole human lives formed in and through the church's disruptive repertoire of disciplines, from singing psalms to daily prayer to communing with Christ at the sacred supper. Thus Calvin positions himself not only *against* monasticism as a critic, but also alongside monasticism as a fellow heir to the church's practical treasury.[14]

To understand fully Calvin's criticism of monasticism, it is necessary first to explicate his view of vows in general and to look at the teaching in his magnum opus, *Institutes of the Christian Religion*.

For Calvin, vows, like wicked pastors and false teachers, serve only one purpose and that is to ensnare humankind, keeping them from their worship of and service to God. Not only has the institutional church often thrown up roadblocks between humans and God, but so have individuals who insist on erecting additional obstacles to be overcome. For Calvin, vows are seen to be particularly heinous when looked at in light of the following: first, "whatever may be required to train men to live pious and holy lives is comprised in the law;" and second, "the Lord, in order better to call us away from inventing new works, has included the entire praise of righteousness in simple obedience to his will" (1254). If these premises are true, says Calvin, then any worship that we devise ourselves, no matter how much it pleases us, is not pleasing to God. God rejects such worship, since

---

13. Calvin, *Institutes of the Christian Religion*, 2:1269. Hereafter cited parenthetically by page number.
14. Boulton, *Life in God*, 12–13.

it is based on false assumptions and oftentimes superstitious beliefs. Thus, any vows that are made "apart from God's express Word" must also be looked at questionably. Between other humans we make promises, writes Calvin, that we think will either please them or that we owe to them, but when we make a promise to God then we are, in fact, making a vow. Therefore, we must be particularly careful about the vows that we make to God. Historically, writes Calvin, men and women have not been careful when making vows to God, they have simply made a vow of anything that came into their minds and/or arose on their lips. Such foolish vow-making is the target of Calvin's ire:

> Hence arose those follies, indeed, monstrous absurdities among the Gentiles, by which they too insolently mocked their gods. And would that even the Christians had not imitated this presumption of theirs! Indeed, they ought not to have done this. But we see that for some centuries nothing has been more usual than this wickedness: whole people everywhere, despising God's law, burned with mad zeal to vow anything that had tickled them in dreams. (1255)

For Calvin, vow-making is a pagan practice, since these people had to make deals with their fickle gods. The Christian God, however, is a God of law and it is the Christian's duty to follow that law so as to please God. Thus, in Calvin's estimation, vow-making is of the utmost seriousness, since it is both a possible offense against God and an imitation of heathen practices.

Calvin now turns to the three criteria that could determine whether a vow is legitimate or "objectionable." First, to whom the vow is made. Second, concerning the one who makes the vow. Third, what someone's intention is in making a vow. Regarding the first criterion, all vows are made to God and God abhors what Calvin calls "self-made religion," that is, all worship that seems right in the eyes of man but is not mandated by God in his Word. Thus, vows that are made as a result of one's own making can never be pleasing to God, for the only pleasing worship is that dictated by God's Word. Thus, "let us not take to ourselves such license as to dare to vow to God that which bears no evidence as to how he may esteem it." Calvin continues, "Let our first precaution in vows, therefore, be never to proceed to any avowal without our conscience first making sure that it attempts nothing rash. But it shall be free of the danger of rashness when it has God going before it and dictating as from his own Word what is good or unprofitable to do" (1256). Calvin concludes that the most appropriate vows, perhaps

The Protestant Reformers

the *only* vows, that we should take are those dictated by God's Word. To make vows rashly and unbiblically is foolishness to Calvin.

Concerning the one who makes the vow, he or she should measure their strength so that God's liberty is not neglected, for "he is a rash man who vows what is either not in his power or conflicts with his calling. And he is ungrateful who despises God's beneficence, which constitutes him lord of all things." Christians must never promise anything to God when they intend to uphold it by their own strength. Further, since humankind has received everything from God's hand, what is his own to vow back to God? Everything that one has comes from goodness and everything that one lacks is withheld by God's justice; thus, to attempt to give to God something that God has already held back is utter foolishness to Calvin. Any vow that one makes to God must already be a gift that God has freely given: "You are to temper your vows to that measure which God by his gift sets for you, lest if you try to go beyond what he allows, in claiming too much for yourself, you cast yourself headlong" (1256). Bad vows of this kind include celibacy, such that "priests, monks, and nuns, forgetful of their own infirmity, think themselves surely capable of celibacy" (1257). Yet, asks Calvin, how do they know that the celibacy that they vow now will continue to be maintained until the end of their life? Instead of celibacy, says Calvin citing Genesis, God has commanded that humankind bear children. Will they be able to "shake off for life that general calling, inasmuch as the gift of continence is more often given for a limited time, as occasion requires," asks Calvin (1257). Since they are going beyond what God expects, they must not ask God to be their helper in this endeavor. Furthermore, those that vow celibacy spurn the very nature that God implanted in them, which is to marry and have children. Calvin affirms the goodness of marriage by reminding his readers that God sanctified marriage, the proof of which is found in Jesus' first miracle occurring at a wedding feast (cf. John 2). For Calvin, those that insist in taking vows of celibacy view what God blesses as "pollution." Without doubt, writes Calvin, "we must vow nothing that may hinder us from serving our calling" (1257). Moreover, since God has already given us every good thing to use for our convenience, to place ourselves under bondage to external things and expect God to find these things acceptable is foolishness. In Calvin's estimation, every good gift that we have been given by God already places us under obligation to him, so that to go above these responsibilities by adding to them is to stand in contempt of God's graciousness.

Reforming the Monastery

Calvin now turns to the third criterion that should determine whether a vow is legitimate or objectionable: "Now I come to my third point: your intention in making a vow is important if you would have God approve it." For Calvin there are four "ends to which our vows ought duly to be directed" (1258). Two of these vows refer to the past and two to the future. Vows in reference to the past fall into two categories: vows that attest our gratitude to God for something that we have received and vows entered into to punish ourselves for offenses that we have committed against God. Calvin calls the first kind of past vows exercises of thanksgiving and the second kind he calls exercises of repentance. A scriptural exercise of thanksgiving for Calvin is the tithes that Jacob vowed to God if he led him back from exile unharmed (cf. Gen 28:20–22). An exercise of repentance, for Calvin, would be as follows: "If anyone should, through the vice of gluttony, fall into any misdeed, nothing will stand in the way of his renouncing all dainty foods for a time in order to chastise his intemperance—doing this with the use of a vow to bind himself with a stricter bond" (1259).

The two future ends to which vows can be directed for Calvin are to make us more cautious in how we live and to arouse us to our Christian duty. Concerning the former: a "man sees himself so prone to a specific vice that in a thing otherwise not bad he cannot prevent himself from falling directly into evil. He will be doing nothing foolish if by vow he cuts off the use of this thing for a time." In regard to the latter, Calvin writes that if a person is lazy or forgetful in fulfilling the "necessary duties of piety," then he should make a vow to "wake up his memory and shake off his laziness." In both cases—that is, with vows of the past or vows of the future—these vows are "lawful, provided they are supported by God's approval, agree with our calling, and are limited to the endowment of grace given us by God" (1259). Having said that these four types of vows are "lawful," Calvin is now ready to offer a conclusion on the nature of lawful and perverse vows.

According to Calvin, all believers share one vow in common, that is the vow made at baptism that they would renounce Satan and would yield themselves "to God's service to obey his holy commandments but not to follow the wicked desires of [the] flesh." This vow receives further sanction at catechism and by partaking in the Lord's Supper and is holy and salutary. Other vows, even when judged lawful, are not to be a daily practice, writes Calvin. Rather, without offering a direct prescription about number or time, Calvin believes that anyone who follows his advice will only enter into "sober and temporary vows." To make too many vows will result in a cheapened religious character by way of repetition and will result in superstition. In short: "If you bind yourself to a perpetual vow, either you will fulfill it with great trouble and tedium, or else, wearied by its long duration, you will one day venture to break it." In other cases, vows are simply perverse and should never be entered into, such as vows regarding fasting, abstinence from wine or meat on certain days and pilgrimages to religious sites. If all of these vows "be examined according to those rules which we have previously laid down, they will be deemed not only empty and fleeting but full of manifest impiety" (1260). Such perverse vows simply make those taking them suppose that they have procured some kind of "exceptional righteousness," thus placing true piety in outward forms and observances, despising others who do not engage in such activity. Without a doubt, Calvin is very much against the taking of lifelong vows that carry any connotation of being superior to expected Christian duty or to the baptismal vows of all Christians. He is not against all vows but only views as valid those vows that are temporary and for the purpose of correcting wrong behavior, showing gratitude to God and vows that punish us for sinning against God.

Having established a theology of vows, Calvin now turns his attention to the relationship of monastic vows and the decline of monastic life over the centuries. He first addresses the argument that the institution of monasticism is legitimate because it has existed since antiquity. Calvin acknowledges the antiquity of monasticism but says that "a far different mode of living once prevailed in monasteries" (1261). In ancient monasteries, the monks slept on the ground; only drank water; ate only bread, vegetables and roots; and abstained bodily from "sumptuous fare and pampering the body." This testimony is trustworthy, believes Calvin, because it has been passed down by reputable authors, including Gregory of Nazianzus, Basil of Caesarea, John Chrysostom, and especially Augustine of Hippo. These monasteries served as "seminaries of the ecclesial order," providing the church with learned clergy and bishops. From the works of Augustine, Calvin can demonstrate that the earliest monks were able to have quite a variation in their ascetical discipline. Thus, there is no real comparison between early Christian and sixteenth-century monasticism, writes Calvin. What was once done out of Christian freedom is now done out of obligation and a spirit of legalism. Whereas earlier monks were a benefit to the church, sixteenth-century monks are a burden due to their idleness. For Augustine, monasticism was "an exercise and aid to those duties of piety enjoined upon all Christians" (1264), but by Calvin's time it was seen as superior to the life of other Christians and was, for all purposes, a clique. In summary, "the character of present-day monasticism is so different that you could scarcely find things more unlike, not to say contrary" (1265). Reformation-era monks, says Calvin, dream up a new piety in order to claim to be more perfect than other believers.

Having established the error of monastic vows and shown that contemporary monasticism was dislike early monasticism, Calvin next turns his attention to the claim that monasticism is a state of perfection. It would appear that in Calvin's time, Roman Catholic theologians were making two claims related to the perfection of the monastic state: 1) that monks were perfect; and 2) that the institution of monasticism led most directly to perfection and was, therefore, a superior form of life. Calvin rejects both understandings since he sees all of Christ's commands as applicable to all Christians. Jesus Christ did not merely advise people to love one's enemies, not seek vengeance, not to swear, etc., but he commanded such behavior for all people. Monastics believe that "a more perfect rule of life can be devised than the common one committed by God to the whole church," but this is simply not true, writes Calvin (1266). In Calvin's time, it seems that some monastics argued that Matthew 19:21 legislated monasticism ("If you would be perfect, go, sell what you possess and give to the poor, and you will have treasure in heaven; and come, follow me"). Calvin's response is simply to remind his readers that the Apostle Paul says that if you give all that you have to the poor and yet do not have love then you are nothing. Furthermore, Calvin explains that when read in context, this passage in no way supports the institution of monasticism, though he acknowledges that some early church fathers did in fact misunderstand the passage and advocate for voluntary poverty.

However, asserts Calvin, in spite of their misunderstanding of this passage, these church fathers did not "establish the kind of perfection afterward fabricated by these hooded Sophists so as to set up a double Christianity" (1268). Whereas Augustine advocated for a monasticism aimed towards love, contemporary monastics do no such thing. Calvin goes so far as to assert that those who enter monastic communities during his age are actually breaking with the church. He asks, "Do they not separate themselves from the lawful society of believers, in adopting a peculiar ministry and a private administration of the sacraments?" (1269). Unlike early Christian monks, though they lived apart from others, they still worshipped with non-monastics and were a part of the people of God. Subsequent monastics built private altars for themselves, breaking the bond of unity. These contemporary monks have "excommunicated themselves from the whole body of the church" and despised the ministry entrusted to all believers by Jesus Christ. In some of his harshest words, Calvin writes that "every monastery existing today . . . is a conventicle of schismatics, disturbing the order of the church and cut off from the lawful society of believers" (1269). Because monastics have set themselves apart from ordinary Christians they have divided the church, which, of course, indicates their unbiblical nature.

In his penultimate salvo against monasticism, Calvin explains how the institutions of widows and deaconesses in the New Testament were not nuns. Before considering this question, however, Calvin summarizes his conclusions thus far. First, ancient monks and contemporary monks have little if anything in common: "Our hooded friends falsely claim the example of the first church in defense of their profession—since they differ from them as much as apes from men" (1270). Second, whatever monastics vow is abominable in God's sight because it creates a "new and forged worship." Third, monks and nuns "invent any mode of life they please without regard for God's call, and without his approval." Fourth, because they bind themselves through false vows to perverted and impious acts of worship, "they are consecrated not to God but to an evil spirit." Calvin also reminds his readers that he has been talking about the institution of monasticism, not about individual monastics. He has been attacking the foundations and principles of monasticism itself and not simply the failings of a few monks or nuns. Nevertheless, should he wish to talk about monastic morals, those too have failed from the earliest Christian centuries to his time. Contemporary monastics are "polluted by all sorts of foul vices" (1269), including factions, hatred, zeal for one's own monastic order and lust: "You will scarcely find one in ten [monasteries] which is not a brothel rather than a sanctuary of chastity" (1270). Despite such gloom, though, Calvin acknowledges that there are still some good monks and nuns hidden among the evil monks and he believes that their brothers and sisters treat them cruelly.

Turning then to the question of whether widows and deaconesses in the New Testament were nuns, Calvin begins by summarizing monastic vows again. He notes that vows were established in an effort to merit God's favor; they bind those taking vows to an invented mode of life without regard for God's call on someone's life; and since they bind one to impious acts, they are vows not consecrated to God but to evil spirits. It seems that Calvin's main issue is with the vow of chastity. He accuses the Roman

Catholic Church of viewing chastity so highly that it is better for a monk or nun to remain continent while tempted beyond what they are able to handle, rather than marry: "They not only admit no moderation or pardon when anyone is found unable to keep his vow, but shamelessly declare that he sins more heinously if he cures the intemperance of his flesh by taking a wife than if he corrupts body and soul by fornication" (1272).

Contemporary monastics argued that the vow of chastity was customary during the time of the apostles. Calvin acknowledges that the Apostle Paul teaches in 1 Timothy 5:11–12 that widows who married after being received into public ministry were violating the pledge of celibacy that they made. Yet, he writes, they took a vow of celibacy "not because they regarded it as something religious of itself . . . but because they could not carry on their function without being their own masters and free of the marriage yoke" (1273). To not remarry because one has taken a so-called lifelong vow is to "cast off God's call" on one's life. For Calvin, God can easily call one into a celibate season of life as well as call one back to the state of marriage. Obedience to one's baptismal vows always trumps one's subsequent vows. Calvin believes that these women only vowed celibacy after being widowed because the work that they undertook could only be accomplished if they remained single and, therefore by necessity, celibate. Further, he believes that the only reason that they subsequently married was that they were unable to bear "the stings of the flesh" (1273).

Similarly, biblical deaconesses are also not nuns, according to Calvin. Whereas nuns spend their time singing songs or offering "unintelligible mumbling" to God, says Calvin, deaconesses "discharge the public ministry of the church toward the poor and strive with all zeal, constancy, and diligence in the task of love" (1274). Like the widows, they did not adopt celibacy because they viewed it as superior to marriage, but chose it in order to serve the church more devotedly. Also like the widows, the deaconesses were not to be received into this order unless they were mature and beyond the age of sixty, as per 1 Timothy 5:9.

Calvin's final attack on the institution of monasticism as it existed in his time has to do with the supposed belief in the binding nature of monastic vows. As seen above, this was one of Martin Luther's most consistent critiques as well. According to Calvin, he has been more than sufficiently clear regarding the oftentimes impious nature of monastic vows. But in order to help those whose consciences are not clear when they break their vows, he offers one last series of explanations. He reminds his readers that those who take unlawful or "improperly conceived vows" are not obligated to keep them since these vows "are of no value before God." Certainly anyone who has taken a hasty vow is allowed to break it in order to live a life more pleasing to God. In fact, Calvin goes so far as to say that this kind of vow *must* be rescinded. Calvin believes that nothing further needs to be said about the unbinding nature of vows since this alone is a sufficient argument for their abolishment. Thus, anyone who has taken such a rash vow not only has the right and obligation to abolish the vow, but is also provided with sufficient reasons for making a defense against the "slanders of the wicked" (1275).

From the foregoing, we can see that John Calvin was not wholly against monasticism in all its forms since he was capable of speaking at times of the goodness of ancient patterns of monasticism. Like Luther, Calvin was certainly against any view of monasticism that implied it was more meritorious or holy than other forms of Christian life and he rejected by and large the concept of permanent monastic vows. At the same time, however, Calvin was capable of speaking positively of monasticism and/or of individual monastics. As cited above, Matthew Boulton goes so far as to suggest that Calvin was not so much against monasticism as he was opposed to the Roman Catholic articulation of monasticism that said that monasticism was a superior form of the Christian life: "Calvin positions himself not only *against* monasticism as a critic, but also alongside monasticism as a fellow heir to the church's practical treasury. He argues that this inheritance belongs as much to the common laity as to monastics."[15] According to Boulton, Calvin, like Martin Luther, simply viewed the monastic life as the life that all Christians should live; that is, the so-called "monastic life" was simply the well-lived Christian life. Boulton rejects the idea that Calvin was some sort of a "crypto-monastic theologian" and concludes, "Calvin did not conceive himself as an heir to a distinctively *monastic* treasury of formative practices, but rather to an even older, distinctively *scriptural and early ecclesial* treasury of such practices" (22). Calvin, along with monasticism in general, viewed the Christian life as primarily a life of training and discipline, "a life of formative education, practical training, and spiritual discipline" (24). According to Boulton, Calvin understood the positive aspects of monasticism to include an emphasis on literacy and education so that the monk could study scriptural and liturgical texts; a daily routine structured around a daily regimen of prayer and worship; regular and frequent chanting of the Psalms; a closely regulated moral life, witnessed by others;

---

15. Boulton, *Life in God*, 13. Hereafter cited parenthetically by page number.

and a governing telos of a life of sanctification and ultimate mystical union with God. This being the case, Boulton argues that Calvin set up Geneva's religious practices along these lines of monastic practice and spirituality.

Like monks and nuns, Calvin also finds the world an inhospitable place for robust Christian formation, but instead of advocating a flight from the world to the monastery, Calvin aspires to transform the whole city into a kind of spiritual and monastic desert. Calvin believes that Christians should adopt a rule of life, "an ascetic rule that begins with 'renouncing our former life,' that is, our 'impiety and worldly' desires" (25). This will set the Christian apart from those not seeking Christian holiness, creating a reformed spiritual life lived in the midst of the ordinary affairs of life. Such a Christian life is a life of self-denial, an ideal historically espoused by and limited to monastics. For Calvin, this reformed Christian life manifests itself in a "reverence and love for God 'which joins us in true holiness with God when we are separated from the iniquities of the world.'" Again, this is not an escape into the desert but a kind of "engaged detachment vis-à-vis the world, a renunciation that involves neither resentment nor retreat" (26). According to Boulton, Calvin believes that the devout Christian engages in a life of Christian formation, characterized by an appropriate contempt of the world, ongoing asceticism, studying the Scriptures and chanting the Psalms in the vernacular, living among and under the watchful, accountable eye of his lay neighbors and the city's consistory. The pious Christian does not flee to the cloister but seeks mystical union with God alongside the whole church, not only among a group of spiritual elites living under humanly fabricated vows. Though Calvin could, at times, be a supporter of monasticism, especially if it aligned with early Christian monasticism, he was at all times a supporter of a robust Christian life. For Calvin, the monastic life is unnecessary if all believers simply live in the fullness of their calling as Christians.

OTHER PROTESTANT REFORMERS

Among the Protestant Reformers, Martin Luther and John Calvin were not the only advocates of doing away with monasticism or, at the least, reforming it along more biblical lines, as they understood it. Ulrich Zwingli, Protestant reformer of Zürich, Switzerland, turned his attention to monasticism as early as January 1523 when he engaged in a disputation with the Roman Catholic, John Faber. The result of this debate was Zwingli's statement commonly known as "The Sixty-Seven Articles" (but in German, *Expositions and Proof of the Articles*). The twenty-seventh article reads, "That all Christians are brothers of Christ and brothers one of another and no one on earth should be called father. Thus orders, sects, and fraternities are untenable." In his exposition of this article, Zwingli writes that the institution of monasticism exists only to make money. In fact, monasteries are a "money-trap," accepting only those who "give enough."[16] Zwingli accuses the monks of only being motivated to pray when paid to do so by those individuals paying for masses for the dead: "They vow poverty, and yet there is no one on earth more wealthy than the monks—and none more avaricious." This is reminiscent of Article 46 which he titles, "Thus it must follow that chanting and loud clamor which lack true devotion and are done only for the sake of reward, either seek the praise of men or material gain." Similarly, Article 33 says that "ill-gotten gain should not be given to temples, cloisters, monk, clerics and nuns, but to the poor, provided it cannot be restored to the rightful owner." Further, as the title to Article 27 states, since no one is to be called "father" or "teacher" except Jesus Christ, then following an abbot is sinful. Particularly, for Zwingli, many orders have come into being merely for the benefit of individuals to be imitators of truly pious men for the purpose of pride and money: "Successive imitators have called themselves followers and disciples of such pious men in order to achieve greater distinction before men and to extract a better profit for their prayers."

Additionally, like Luther and Calvin, Zwingli argues against monasticism on the basis of the vows that a monk or a nun is expected to take. In his *Commentary on True and False Religion*, Zwingli argues that the taking of some vows, including monastic vows, is impious and foolish. That monastics take the vows of chastity, poverty, and obedience shows clearly the depth of their unwise and contrived zeal. Concerning chastity, nowhere in Scripture, writes Zwingli, does God demand that the holiest of his chosen people abstain from marriage. Quite the contrary, God calls some to marriage and others to celibacy. Either station of life is pleasing to God, thus, "all vows of chastity are impious." For Zwingli, God decides who will be rich and who will poor; therefore, to vow poverty is pointless. Moreover, we are all to be poor in spirit (Matt 5:3), so a special vow is unnecessary. That monastics vow obedience to their superior runs counter to the biblical admonition that we owe obedience to all people. For Zwingli, this is

---

16. All quotations are from Pipkin, "Zwingli, the Laity and the Orders."

especially clear in Matthew 5:41: "If someone forces you to go one mile, go with him two miles." More importantly, if we are to vow obedience to anyone, it should be to God, not to a monastic superior. All things considered, Zwingli believes that monastic vows are ultimately used to avoid and evade God's divine laws and will. In Zwingli's view, monasticism amounts to injustices, sin, hypocrisy, fraud, profiteering, and deceit.

Andreas Bodenstein von Carlstadt, an extreme German reformer and former colleague of Martin Luther at the University of Wittenberg, also argues against monasticism by offering a translation and commentary on Numbers 30, which has to do with the taking of vows. Though the earliest version of this commentary was written in Latin and spoke harshly about alleged abuses in monastic houses, the subsequent German edition of 1522 addresses the issues of vows in a much more balanced manner, especially in the lengthy preface. Carlstadt's opening paragraph summarizes well his eventual conclusion: "This booklet concludes, on the basis of biblical, Christian laws . . . that priests, monks, and nuns may and ought to marry and enter upon the marital estate with a good conscience. . . . It advises above-named persons to cast off their deceitful living habits along with gowns and cowls and to enter upon a true Christian life."[17] Carlstadt begins by asserting that anyone who makes a vow needs to do so with wisdom, for to make an unwise vow angers God and causes those who make the vows to be angry with God, thus impeding one's spiritual development. Further, Moses, writes Carlstadt, says that a person who does not make a vow or who refuses to make a vow does not sin. It is not a sin *not* to make a vow, but once a vow is made it is a sin to not live into the vows. Therefore, a person should not be too hasty in making vows. Contrary to the teaching of Moses, believes Carlstadt, is the Roman Catholic Church's willingness to encourage the making of vows in a hasty and frequent manner. Further, Carlstadt asserts that these vows encouraged by the Roman Catholic Church are illegitimate vows since they are made to the church and not to God. According to Carlstadt, the scriptures teach that all vows have to be made to God and to God alone. The Bible calls believers away from vows made to anyone other than God.

In Carlstadt's estimation, the taking of vows at this time amounted to making a vow at least to God *and* a saint, but possibly only to a saint. Either kind of vow is a sin for Carlstadt. He ridicules the fact that those who were sick, for example, would pray to a saint for healing, and promise that if the

---

17. Carlstadt, *Essential Carlstadt*, 52. Hereafter cited parenthetically by page number.

saint healed them then they would give something in return. For example, "You say that you called on St. Sebastian in your distress and that you were able to recover from the plague. Another says that he promised to St. Gertrude or St. Nicholas an image made of silver when he was floating in the water but was rescued" (58). Such vows, writes Carlstadt, are sinful and demonstrate that one is not making a vow to God but to the church by way of a saint, and that is a sin. This leads the German reformer to conclude that

> the one acts contrary to the first commandment of God who in divine works and matters seeks out a saint or angel besides God. Monks and nuns do this. They not only join themselves to God, but besides God to a saint through oaths and vows; because of this they have an uncircumcised and divided heart. By this everyone can readily conclude that their worship, honoring, vows, and covenants are displeasing to God and harmful to them. (65)

He continues by saying that if one makes a vow to God and a saint, then God is being robbed of his honor and new gods are being created in God's place. Turning to the specific example of chastity, Carlstadt, like Luther, says that it is a gift of God, and one can only remain celibate if God has given one the gift of celibacy. A man or woman who is unable to remain celibate naturally will not be able to be celibate simply because he or she took a vow. Moreover, Carlstadt notes that even if God has given one the gift of celibacy that does not mean that one should take a vow, much less a vow to God and a saint. Monks and nuns, he writes, do not take vows of celibacy to God only but to God and a saint: "I ask monks and nuns (who vow chastity to God and a patron such as St. Clare or Benedict) what they are doing. With my limited understanding, I reckon they should do one of two things. They must ask God and their patron to bestow all chastity or that they might keep them in the purity that was bestowed. But they must attribute their chastity to God and the saint" (68). To do so, concludes Carlstadt, is to sin and promise an evil and to "displease and alienate God" (70).

From this we see that Zwingli and Carlstadt, like Luther and Calvin, were all primarily against Roman Catholic monasticism because it involved the taking of lifelong vows. Such vow-taking was either done rashly and hastily and, therefore, against God's commands, or they were not actually vows to God but vows before saints or monastic superiors. As well, there is a strong sense in the writings of the Protestant Reformers that the institution of monasticism replaced the biblical teaching of justification by faith. For these reasons, the Reformers (mostly) rejected monasticism but the

Reforming the Monastery

way still seemed to be left open for some sort of a reformed monasticism, something that would only come about in later centuries.

TWO

The Anglican Tradition

Early Anglican Authors

In 1536, King Henry VIII of England, along with his chief minister, Thomas Cromwell, commenced what has come to be known as the dissolution or suppression of the monasteries in the British Isles. Though calls for the suppression of monasteries had been issued since at least the fourteenth century, it was only between 1536 and 1540 that over eight hundred monasteries were dissolved. The nature of the dissolution is described well by Joyce Youings:

> The Dissolution of the Monasteries in England and Wales in the reign of Henry VIII was an act of resumption, a restoration to secular uses of land and other endowments provided over many centuries . . . for the support of houses of regular clergy and nuns. What was achieved in the 1530s was the reversal of a series of acts of donation, but with the important proviso that all of the property passed in the first instance not to the original donors or their heirs and assigns but to the Crown. By various means . . . the monastic lands became vested in the king, to be at his absolute disposal.[1]

Regardless of Henry's motives (and there are many theories), institutional monastic life in England was, more or less, absent for the next three hundred years. I say "more or less" because there are many examples of forms of religious life that may, in fact, be thought of as monastic, even if the originators and/or participants did not view their lives as traditionally monastic.

1. Youings, *Dissolution of the Monasteries*, 13.

Reforming the Monastery

Many of these proposals never resulted in concrete manifestations, but monastic sentiments were frequently expounded. As the novelist Joseph Henry Shorthouse asked in his novel *John Inglesant* from 1881, "What was this life of holiness that men ought to lead? Could it be followed in the world? Or must he retire to some monastic solitude to cultivate it; and was it certain that it would flourish even there?"[2] Such questioning motivated many of the Anglicans who sought the return of monasticism to England. In particular, those who suggested that Anglican monasteries should be founded for women were often doing so for the express purpose of providing some place for widows, those deemed unable to marry, and "spinsters" to reside. Others thought that Protestant monasteries were needed because of the usefulness of these monasteries to society as a whole, though there were overtly religious motivations for founding Protestant monasteries too. An example of the former would be Edmund Burke (d. 1797), who, in his *Reflections on the Revolution in France*, questioned why those responsible for the French Revolution would seek to rid the country of monasteries. For Burke, the monasteries were ideal institutions for the distribution of benevolent forms of charity. He was insistent that the state could not serve the public good in this manner as well as the monasteries had always done. Burke did not care that the monks were, by his judgment, lazy, occupied themselves too much in singing, or were superstitious; they were the best "corporations" for the distribution of necessary aid.[3]

An example of those who founded a monastery for overt religious reasons would be the Ferrar family. In 1625, Mary Ferrar purchased a dilapidated house with an abandoned chapel in the small Huntingdonshire parish of Little Gidding. Soon thereafter, her sons Nicholas and John joined her, along with John's wife, Bathsheba, and their many children, as well as by her daughter, Susanna, along with her husband, John Collett, and their sixteen children. Nicholas, a one-time member of the English Parliament and ordained deacon in the Church of England, was the primary spiritual head of the community. The small community remained a family affair and was dedicated to unceasing prayer (as there was always someone at prayer) and followed a fairly strict routine, including Sabbath observance and the recitation of the daily offices, beginning at 4 a.m. in the summer and 5 a.m. in the winter. Outside of the community, the family engaged in the education and care of poor local children and the production of books for

2. Shorthouse, *John Inglesant*, 197.
3. Burke, *Reflections on the Revolution in France*, 158–64.

The Anglican Tradition

spiritual edification for both children and adults. Though certainly monastic in spirit, A. L. Maycock, biographer of Nicholas Ferrar and the Little Gidding community, adamantly writes that the "rule of Little Gidding was in no sense monastic. There is no evidence whatever that Nicholas had any idea or intention of restoring the religious (i.e. the monastic) life within the Church of England."[4] Yet the lifestyle of the community was "monastic" enough to cause a group of Puritans to publish a booklet about the community in 1641, titled "The Arminian Nunnery: Or, A Briefe Description and Relation of the late erected Monasticall Place, called the Arminian Nunnery at little Gidding in Huntington-Shire." This offensive pamphlet was based on a letter of Edward Lenton, who visited Little Gidding in 1634, to Thomas Hetley. In this letter, Lenton calls the community the "Nunnery at Gidding" and refers to Nicholas' female relatives as "the Nuns of Gidding." We also learn from this letter, however, that in their defense, Nicholas said to Lenton that "the name of Nuns was odious" and that they "had made no vows." In short, Little Gidding "was a small community combining the 'rule of a Religious house with the ordinary routine of domestic life.'"[5]

At the same time, John Bramhall, Archbishop of Armagh who died in 1663, spoke positively of the institution of monasticism. When writing about the dissolution of the monasteries under Henry VIII, Bramhall says that he "shall deal clearly, and declare what I conceive to be the judgment of moderate English Protestants concerning the act." He continues,

> First, we fear that covetousness had a great oar in the boat, and that sundry of the principal actors had a greater aim at the *goods* of the Church, than at the *good* of the Church.... So as monasteries were moderated in their number, and in their revenues; so as the monks were restrained from meddling between the pastor and his flock ... ; so as the abler sort, who are not taken up with higher studies or weightier employments, were inured to bestow their spare hours from their devotions in some profitable labour for the public good ... ; so as the vow of perpetual celibate [*sic*] were reduced ... ; so as their blind obedience were more enlightened, and secured by some certain rules and bounds; so as their mock poverty ... were changed into a competent maintenance; and, lastly, so as all opinion of satisfaction and supererogation were removed;

---

4. Maycock, *Nicholas Ferrar of Little Gidding*, 197.

5. Hill, "Refuge from Men," 110. Hill is quoting from Carter, *Nicholas Ferrar*, 97. The following is greatly influenced by Hill's article; Legg, *English Church Life*, 281–91; and the Earl of Wicklow, "The Monastic Revival in the Anglican Communion."

Reforming the Monastery

> I do not see why monasteries might not agree well enough with reformed devotion.[6]

Thus, Bramhall can imagine a kind of monasticism that avoids what he believes to be the traps that late medieval and Reformation-era monasteries had fallen into. For Bramhall, a reformed monasticism is desirable. Other seventeenth-century ecclesiastics who regretted the loss of monasticism in the Church of England were William Sancroft, Archbishop of Canterbury (d. 1693), and Herbert Thorndike, Canon of Westminster Abbey (d. 1672). Sancroft, while Dean of St. Paul's in London from 1664 to 1668, gave spiritual direction to twelve women living monastically in a convent in London. This information, preserved in the autobiography of Fr. Bede of St. Simon Stock (born Walter Joseph Travers, in 1619), reads,

> Let me conclude my narrative by saying that the Protestants in England have neither monks nor nuns of their creed, and what efforts they have made in this direction have proved unsuccessful. In my time there were about twelve Protestant ladies of gentle birth and considerable means who had an idea of founding a convent in London. Submitting their plan to the then Dean of St. Paul's, now Archbishop of Canterbury, they secured his approbation, as well as his services, as their director and ghostly father.

This living arrangement failed, however, when the "Abbess" went to Flanders to study the Rule of Benedict in one of the exiled English Benedictine abbeys, and instead of returning to London, she converted to Roman Catholicism and married.[7] Thorndike, when discussing celibacy, writes that

> it is advised by our Lord in the gospel; and therefore hath the promise of His grace, to them that embrace it as Christians: it is in the next place to be said, that it is most acceptable to God, and honourable to Christianity. But as the best things, when they are corrupted, turn the worst; so is the danger greatest, now the world is come into the Church, that they, who choose the most sublime course for low and mean reasons, will not be able to hold their choice. And therefore, seeing the whole order and course of monastical life is introduced by the Church, and rather by sufferance than by law, the want of it cannot be a bar to the salvation of them, that live in the Church that hath it not. But seeing it is a perfection

---

6. Bramhall, *Works of the Most Reverend Father in God, John Bramhall, D.D.*, 1:119–20.
7. Travers, "Autobiography of Father Bede of St. Simon Stock," 275–76.

to Christianity, it is certainly a blot in the reformation which we profess, that we are without it.[8]

For Thorndike, then, monasticism should exist so that those with a legitimate calling to celibacy may live their life in this manner. In this way, monasticism exists "by sufferance than by law." That is, it exists as a form of life and a manner of devotion to those whom God called and not as right established by church law. In Thorndike's theology, monasticism is akin to other forms of Christian living, especially marriage, and is not a superior form of life. Monasticism should exist to provide shelter for those with a calling to celibacy, just as marriage exists for those not called to celibacy.

Similarly, in 1707, Thomas Ken (d. 1711), Anglican bishop of Bath and Wells, in a letter to Thomas Smith, refers to "two good Virgins beyond Bristol where there is a kind of nunnery."[9] These two women, Mary and Anne Kemeys, upon the death of their mother in 1683, retired to a home where "they established a kind of nunnery or Anglican sisterhood, of the Little Gidding type." Both sisters died in 1708 and a marble tablet in their memory in the parish church of Clapton-in-Gordano refers to the sisters as "wise virgins," "who both chose the better part." Further, John Duncon, in his early twentieth-century biography of Lettice Falkland, who died in 1646, writes of Falkland's desire that "places for the education of Gentlewomen and for the retirement of Widows" would be constructed so that women would have "opportunities to serve the Lord without distraction." Duncon says that Falkland's desire was based upon "Nicholas Ferrar's 'Protestant Nunnery' at Little Gidding."[10] Though Falkland herself does not use the term *nunnery*, it would seem that her desire for such homes approaches something like a monastery. Robert Burton, vicar of Oxford University who died in 1640, speaks about the benefits of the life of virginity. Though he seems less inclined to suggest such a life for men, he does say that individuals who remain virgins, contrary to missing out on life's luxuries, do benefit greatly from such a lifestyle because they can easily endure the "inconveniences, irksomeness, [and] solitariness" of the unmarried life. For women, in particular, Burton writes that "methinks sometime or other, amongst so many rich Bachelors, a benefactor should be found to build a monastical College for old, decayed, deformed, or discontented maids to live together in, that have lost their first loves, or otherwise miscarried,

---

8. Thorndike, *Theological Works of Herbert Thorndike*, 5:570–71.
9. All quotations are from Plumptre, *Life of Thomas Ken, D.D.*, 2:167–69.
10. Duncon, *Lady Lettice, Vi-Countess Falkland*, 27–28.

or else are willing howsoever to lead a single life."[11] Apart from the misogynistic tone, in essence Burton is making a case for a kind of monastic life for these women. Thomas Fuller (d. 1661), Anglican priest and church historian, in his *Church History of Britain*, speaks favorably of monasteries for women, saying that prior to the Reformation, monasteries afforded women the opportunity to attain a higher perfection than that afforded by the seventeenth-century Anglican Church.

On September 3, 1659, the writer John Evelyn wrote to the philosopher Robert Boyle that he wished to gather a group of like-minded men to "join together in society, and resolve upon some orders and œconomy, to be mutually observed." Evelyn's plan was to purchase thirty to forty acres of land near London and to construct a common dormitory on the land with "apartments or cells" consisting of "a small bedchamber, an outward room, a closet, and a private garden, somewhat after the manner of the Carthusians." The building would also have "a pretty chapel."[12] Not only was the architecture to be reminiscent of a medieval religious order, but the diet was similar as well: "One meal a day, of two dishes only ... of plain and wholesome meat; a small refection at night." Evelyn then wrote up a set of "orders" for the society, which are worth quoting in full:

> At six in summer prayers in the chapel. To study till half an hour after eleven. Dinner in the refectory till one. Retire till four. Then called to conversation (if the weather invite) abroad, else in the refectory; this never omitted but in case of sickness. Prayers at seven. To bed at nine. In the winter the same, with some abatements for the hours, because the nights are tedious, and the evening's conversation more agreeable; this in the refectory. All play interdicted, *sans* bowls, chess, &c. Every one to cultivate his own garden. One month in spring a course in the elaboratory on vegetables, &c. In the winter a month on other experiments. Every man to have a key of the elaboratory, pavilion, library, repository, &c. Weekly fast. Communion once every fortnight, or month at least. No stranger easily admitted to visit any of the Society, but upon certain days weekly, and that only after dinner. Any of the Society may have his commons to his apartment, if he will not meet in the refectory, so it be not above twice a week. Every Thursday shall be a music meeting at conversation hours. Every person of the Society shall render some public account of his studies weekly if thought fit, and

---

11. Burton, *Anatomy of Melancholy*, 3:258.

12. The Carthusians were founded in 1084 by Bruno of Cologne in southeastern France. They are known for their extreme asceticism and rigid enclosure.

especially shall be recommended the promotion of experimental knowledge, as the principal end of the institution. There shall be a decent habit and uniform used in the college. One month in the year may be spent in London, or any of the Universities, or in a perambulation for the public benefit, &c., with what other orders shall be thought convenient, &c.[13]

Though not strictly a monastery but rather a center to promote "experimental knowledge," one is forced to notice that Evelyn's plans are very monastic, so much so that he himself compares the facility's arrangement to a Carthusian charterhouse.

In her 1662 play, *The Convent of Pleasure*, Margaret Cavendish writes about a woman, appropriately named Lady Happy, who, upon the death of her father, enters a monastery because she believes that even marriage to a virtuous man is a greater limitation than living life in a monastery. As already noted, many argued for the presence of monasteries so that women, writes Edward Chamberlayne in 1671, could live as "sober, pious, [and] elder Virgins and Widdows [sic]." Chamberlayne (d. 1703) writes that he desires to found a college, "or Protestant Monastery," "for the education of young ladies, under the government of some grave matrons, who shall resolve to lead the rest of their dayes [sic] in a single retired religious life." To this effect, Chamberlayne sought someone who could inform him of monastic "Rules and Constitution."[14] Elizabeth Godolphin, Anglican laywoman, wrote her friend, the aforementioned John Evelyn, that the "want of Monasteryes and pyous [sic] Recesses obliged her to marry." Godolphin, while in Paris, visited women's monasteries and found them to be "holy Institutions."[15] The great feminist writer Mary Astell (d. 1731) proposed in her *Serious Proposal to the Ladies* that monasteries should be erected so that there would be in improvement in the education of women. She writes, "[A]s to the Proposal it is to erect a *Monastery* . . . and such as shall have a double aspect, being not only a Retreat from the World for those who desire that advantage, but likewise, an institution and previous discipline, to fit us [women] to do the greatest good in it."[16] Likewise, Astell's friend Mary Wortley Montagu, in a letter dated October 20, 1752, confesses to her daughter that she had been attracted to the proposition of founding

---

13. All quotations are from Evelyn, *Diary and Correspondence*, 3:116–19.
14. *Correspondence of John Cosin*, Part II, 384–85.
15. Evelyn, *Life of Mrs. Godolphin by John Evelyn of Wotton Esq.*, 81 and 121.
16. Astell, *Serious Proposal to the Ladies*, 73. Italics in the original.

Reforming the Monastery

an "English monastery" where she would serve as the "lady abbess."[17] In 1698, Anglican clergyman George Wheler published a large volume titled *The Protestant monastery: or, Christian oeconomicks: Containing directions for the religious conduct of a family*, in which he argues that such institutions would be profitable for society, women especially. One biographer of Wheler states that Wheler was "anxious for the foundation of monasteries on purely protestant principles, or rather for the establishment of institutions where, at a small expense, persons of good family, superior attainments, and decidedly Christian character, might be enabled to devote themselves to the service of God."[18] Wheler believes that erecting "Convents for the retirement of single Men" would not be too useful. Yet, he believes that convents for women are most necessary: "Convents for single Women seem more convenient, if not necessary for all times and Countries, and are by far less dangerous, since no considerable detriment can be expected from them, if due regard be had in composing the Rules of their Institution. . . . Tho' such Monasteries as these, and thus duly ordered, would undoubtedly be both a reputation to the Church, and Advantagious to the Nation."[19] In Wheler's view, these nuns would be allowed to marry and remain in society, though enclosed in their own homes.

A more robust imagining of the restoration of monasticism into the Church of England came from Wheler's contemporary, Edward Stephens (d. 1706), a pamphleteer and moral reformer. In his first tract, *A Discourse Concerning the Original of the Powder-Plot* (1674), Stephens argues that the laxity among Church of England clergy was driving committed (as opposed to nominal) Anglicans to join various sects, thus weakening the Church of England's resistance to Roman Catholicism. Having founded the Society for the Reformation of Manners in the 1690s, Stephens published, in 1696, a work titled *Asceticks: or, The Heroick Piety and Virtue of the Ancient Christian Anchorets and Coenobites: Exemplary Asceticks*, in which he writes the following:

> Monkery is not only rendered Odious, as of it self [sic], but also as a part of Popery. And, indeed, if we imagin [sic] all that is believed or practised by the Church of Rome to be Popery, it may be so: but then we shall leave little of true Christianity for the Reformation: But if what is true Christianity be not Popery, than neither

17. Montagu, *Works of the Right Honourable Lady Mary Worley Montagu*, 178.
18. "Biography: Rev. Sir George Wheeler," 333.
19. Wheler, *Protestant Monastery*, 14–19.

The Anglican Tradition

is Monkery, as some are pleased to call Monastick Life; And that it is not only true Christianity, but the Practice of it in the greatest Perfection that Mortals are capable of, I am apt to think will be very plain to any who will consider what here follows with an unprejudiced and competent Judgment.[20]

Also, sometime after 1700, Edwards wrote a short tract titled *The More Excellent Way: or a Proposal of a Compleat Work of Charity*, subtitled as

For the Accommodation of some Devout Women, with such mean but convenient Habitation, Work, Wages, and Relief, that they may have Time and Strength for the Worship of God, both in Publick and Private, and Freedom of Mind for Meditation and Religious Exercises, while their Hands are Imploy'd for Maintenance of the Body; and that while they enjoy the Benefit of such Accommodations for their own Souls, their Benefactors, and the Church and Nation, may be benefitted by their Constant Prayers.

Though he imagines that women living in their homes will accomplish much of this, Stephens is also open to creating a "Seminary of Piety and Virtue, for such single Persons as want no Accommodations of this World" and who "will be Conformable to the Orders of the House." Stephens was so insistent on the reinstitution of monasticism into the Church of England that he also translated Athanasius' *Life of Anthony* and published, for the Religious Society of Single Women, a short work called, *A Letter to a Lady, Concerning the due Improvement of her Advantages of Celibacie, Portion, and Maturity of Age and Judgment: Which may serve indifferently for Men under the same Circumstances*. As in his other works, Stephens here too makes a case for the monastic life, at least for women: "The State and Condition of Celibacie, whether of Virginity or Widow-hood, when it comes to be Voluntary, and of Choice and Preference ... hath the Approbation of our Saviour, of the Holy Scriptures, and hath always been esteemed very Honourable in the Christian Church, and believ'd to be Matter of great Reward hereafter."[21] Despite his desire to see women's monasticism reinstituted in England, Stephens was without a doubt a devout clergyman of the Church of England, stating in a letter to the Archbishop of Canterbury, John Tillotson, on February 21, 1694, that he strives to "avoid giving Offence to any, but especially to the Church of England." As evidenced throughout this chapter, not only laypersons, but many Church of England clergymen

---

20. Stephens, *Asceticks*, 4.
21. Stephens, *Letter to a Lady*, 3–4.

argued for the existence of the institution of monasticism. For example, Francis Atterbury (d. 1732), bishop of Rochester, in his *Maxims, reflections and observations, divine, moral and political*, states that the dissolution of the monasteries under Henry VIII in the sixteenth century was "the great Blemish of our Reformation."[22]

Yet again, it was not only clergy that lamented the loss of monasteries in England. In 1727, Daniel Defoe, author of *Robinson Crusoe* and *Moll Flanders*, published *The Protestant Monastery; or, A Complaint against the Brutality of the present Age*, in which he argued for the erection of a monastery where the poor could live in some form of comfort and would avoid being a burden to their family or place a drain on public charities. Gilbert Burnet, Anglican bishop of Salisbury, wrote in 1734 that "something like monasteries without vows, would be a glorious design."[23] Another Anglican writing in favor of monasticism was Samuel Wesley. Wesley, a friend of Daniel Defoe, was a poet and the father of John and Charles Wesley, founders of the Methodists. In his *Letter Concerning the Religious Societies* (written in 1699 but published in 1724), in defense of the "societies" being founded by his sons, Wesley says that these "religious societies" are of no harm to the church, rather they are of great advantage to the church as were the earliest Christian societies, such as those spoken about by Tertullian. Wesley then offers a positive assessment of monasteries, which merits an extended quotation:

> I know few good men but lament that, after the destruction of monasteries [under Henry VIII, in the sixteenth century], there were not some societies founded in their stead, but reformed from their errors, and reduced to the primitive standard. None who have but looked into our own church history can be ignorant how highly instrumental such bodies of men as these were to the first planting and propagating Christianity amongst our forefathers. 'Tis notorious that the first monks wrought honestly for their livings, and only met together at the hours of prayer, and necessary refection, as do most of those in the eastern countries to this day: and those who read the exemplary piety of the old British monks, and what indefatigable pains they took, and what hazards they ran, in the conversion of our heathen ancestors, as well as how stoutly they withstood the early encroachments of Rome, cannot but entertain an extraordinary opinion of them, and will be apt to

---

22. Atterbury, *Maxims, reflections and observations, divine, moral and political*, 13.
23. Burnet, *History of His Own Time*, 915.

judge charitably of their great austerities and ascetic way of living, though, perhaps, we may be in the right, when we think they were in some things mistaken.... It will be owned a desirable thing that we had among us some places wherein those who are religiously disposed might have the liberty for a time of voluntary retirement; that they might escape the world. . . . This was once practiced, with great applause of all good men, by Mr. Farrar [of Little Gidding].... But if this should not be practicable, at least generally, by men of trade and business, though of never so devout inclinations, I see nothing that could come nearer it than these religious societies. The design of that excellent person, Archbishop [Thomas] Cranmer, to have founded so many collegiate churches out of the broken monasteries, to consist of some laity, as well as clergy, seems to have had something in it of the same nature (though in a higher degree) with that of these Christian societies now erected, namely, to make a stand for religion and virtue, so many redoubts against an encroaching world, where any might receive counsel and advice, who addressed themselves unto them.[24]

For Samuel Wesley, there were the good monasteries of the early church, especially in England, followed by Cranmer's good collegiate churches, and now, in his own time, the good religious societies being formed under the guidance of his own sons. Though Wesley is clearly not making the case for the full restoration of monasticism in eighteenth-century England, he certainly is able to think highly of the institution of monasticism itself.

Like Wesley, William Cuningham of Edinburgh thought so highly of the institution of monasticism that he wrote a proposal to the Anglican canon of Durham, Thomas Sharp, in 1737 suggesting that a woman's monastery should be founded for "Ladies of Quality, and Gentlewomen, of Great Britain." The letter that accompanies the proposal asks that "a Nunnery of Protestant religious and virtuous persons, well born, of the female sex, conforming themselves to the worship of the Church of England, as by law established" be considered. Cuningham claims that he is writing on behalf of some "well-disposed persons" and even asks Sharp to take this proposal, should he find it agreeable, to the bishop of Durham, since Cuningham thinks that the first convent should be founded in the diocese of Durham. This monastery would not be like a Roman Catholic convent "since these ladies are by means to come under vows, but left at liberty to quit the nunnery." Though happy to do all he can to "make any persons better or happier

---

24. Clarke, *Memoirs of the Wesley Family*, 126–27.

than they are," Sharp responds thoroughly to Cuningham's letter, ultimately rejecting the proposal.[25] Church of Ireland bishop and philosopher George Berkeley (d. 1746), in a letter to John James (a friend of Berkeley and a convert to Roman Catholicism), says that he believes that a "monastery... receiving only grown persons of approved piety, learning, and a contemplative turn, would be a great means of... brightening up the face of religion in our Church." Those who join such a monastery, thinks Berkeley, should not take perpetual vows that would result "in a Popish convent."[26] The famous spiritual writer William Law (d.1761) also suggested that individuals could enter the monastic life:

> Persons of either sex... desirous of perfection, should unite themselves into little societies professing voluntary poverty, virginity, retirement, and devotion, living upon bare necessities, that some might be relieved by their charities and all be blessed with their prayers and benefited by their example; or if for want of this, they should practice the same manner of life in as high a degree as they could by themselves, such persons would be so far from being chargeable with any superstition or blind devotion that they might be justly said to restore that piety which was the boast and glory of the church when its greatest Saints were alive.[27]

Like Defoe, novelist Samuel Richardson (d. 1761), in his epistolary novel *The History of Sir Charles Grandison,* has the title character affirm Protestant monastic institutions when he writes that "we want to see established in every county, *Protestant Nunneries,* in which single women, of small or no fortunes, might live with all manner of freedom, under such regulations as it would be a disgrace for a modest or good woman not to comply with, were she absolutely on her own hands; and to be allowed to quit it whenever they pleased."[28] With Berkeley, Richardson does not imagine that these women will take permanent vows; rather, they will have the liberty at the end of every two or three years to renew their vows.

Not only did Anglican authors of this period imagine that women should not take permanent, lifelong monastic vows, but they believed that the women should also engage in non-contemplative acts of mercy. In *Blackwood's Edinburgh Magazine,* an anonymous contributor wrote a small

25. Sharp, *Life of John Sharp,* 2:281–83.
26. Berkeley, *Works of George Berkeley,* 4:530.
27. Law, *Serious Call to a Devout and Holy Life,* 131.
28. Richardson, *History of Sir Charles Grandison,* 203.

entry titled "Protestant Sisters of Charity." In this piece, dated November 1, 1825, the author talks about a friend of his who is desirous of offering medical care to his parishioners but recognizes that this is quite difficult given that these poor live far from the town where a surgeon resides. As well, the surgeon spends most days attending to the town's wealthier citizens while allowing the poor to suffer. This friend wondered if "it was possible to procure a few women of a superior order to the generality of nurses" who, as well, would be "animated with religion." This order of nurses would be for Protestantism a religious order of sisters of charity in imitation of the Roman Catholic "Sœurs de Charité" that the author's friend encountered during a visit to Flanders. The Roman Catholic nuns, a "singular and useful order of Nuns," worked in the hospitals and were strictly motivated by their religion, a superior motivator when compared with medical or scientific zeal. Given that these sisters of charity would offer such useful employment, the anonymous author concludes,

> Let the Church, or if not, let that class of Christians in whom, above all others, religion is not a mere Sunday ceremony, but the daily and hourly principle of their thoughts and actions . . . join, and found an order of women like the Sisters of Charity in Catholic countries; let them be selected for good plain sense, kindness of disposition, indefatigable industry, and deep piety.[29]

It would seem that the anonymous author was Alexander Dallas, an Anglican priest who had served in the Napoleonic Wars. In 1826, he published his *Protestant Sisters of Charity; a Letter Addressed to the Lord Bishop of London*, where he goes into greater detail about this plan, providing almost a kind of rule for these Sisters of Charity.

Finally, Robert Southey (d. 1843), English poet and author, advocates for monasteries in his *Sir Thomas More: Or, Colloquies on the Progress and Prospects of Society*. The work is cast as a conversation between the sixteenth-century martyred Roman Catholic statesman Thomas More and Montesinos (that is, Southey). During a discussion on the Reformation, More asserts that "hermits, as well as monks . . . have been useful in their day." Montesinos agrees and replies, "I consider the dissolution of the Religious Houses as the greatest evil that accompanied the Reformation." Southey then takes the opportunity to have More reveal that he believes that the pre-Reformation monasteries were certainly in need of reform. He says, "Take from such communities their irrevocable vows, their onerous

---

29. "Protestant Sisters of Charity," 734.

laws, their ascetic practices; cast away their mythology, and with it the frauds and follies connected therewith, and how beneficial would they then be found! What opportunities would they afford to literature, what aid to devotion, what refuge to affliction, what consolation to humanity!" Montesinos could not agree more whole-heartedly and replies, "And what relief to society, which, as it becomes more crowded in all its walks, and as education and intelligence are more and more diffused, must in every succeeding generation feel more pressingly the want of such institutions! Considering the condition of single women in the middle classes, it is not speaking too strongly to assert, that the establishment of protestant nunneries, upon a wise plan and liberal scale, would be the greatest benefit that could possibly be conferred upon these kingdoms." For Southey, "There is nothing Romish, nothing superstitious, nothing fanatical" in these religious houses.[30] Thus, up to the middle of the nineteenth century, there was a consistent espousing that the Church of England could benefit from the presence of monastic institutions. Though several individuals made an effort at creating concrete monastic houses, none of them met with success. English Roman Catholics during this time, on the other hand, were quite active in opening monasteries for men and women, though they were all located outside of England. Caroline Bowden has compiled a list of at least twenty-six of these houses, most founded in the first half of the seventeenth century, many of which returned to England in 1794–95. The absence of Anglican monastic houses in England, however, changed with the arrival of the Oxford Movement.

John Keble and Richard Hurrell Froude

The Oxford Movement (also known as Tractarianism) originated among a group of Oxford University tutors and fellows in 1833. At its heart, the movement was an effort to direct the Church of England back towards a more deliberate catholic orientation in both practice and theology (i.e., adopting those practices characteristic of the first nineteen centuries of Christian history), though it also espoused a strong political ideology and emphasis on social justice. C. Brad Faught writes, "The Oxford Movement . . . posed deep and far-reaching questions about the nature of the relationship between church and state, the catholic heritage of the Church

---

30. Southey, *Sir Thomas More*, 2:35–36 and 239.

The Anglican Tradition

of England, and the Church's social responsibility."[31] In orientation, as R. David Cox notes, the "Oxford Movement presented not so much a system of doctrine as an approach to churchmanship. . . . [The leaders] sought to revivify the concept of the Anglican *via media* as a middle road between Roman Catholicism and Protestantism, and make it real in the lives of the faithful."[32] The origin of the Oxford Movement is traditionally dated to July 14, 1833, when John Keble (d. 1866), Oxford professor, poet, and Anglican priest, preached a sermon at St. Mary's Church, Oxford, titled "National Apostasy." In this sermon, Keble warns the Church of England that it must not be like the Israelites, who failed to acknowledge God as their true king while allowing the temporal kings to direct the nation into apostasy: "God forbid, that any Christian land should ever, by her prevailing temper and policy, revive the memory and likeness of Saul, or incur a sentence of reprobation like his." Keble and the earliest Tractarians (including primarily John Henry Newman, Edward Pusey, and Richard Hurrell Froude), believed that the state-supported Church of England had already begun to go the way of unfaithful Israel and it was time to restore the Church of England to her rightful place in society. As the movement quickly gained momentum, its theological agenda was composed primarily of reinstituting/reintroducing traditional, catholic church practices, including monasticism. As Ruth Kenyon writes, "The revival of the 'Religious' or Monastic Life in the English Church was an aspiration of the Tractarians from the very beginning."[33] A contemporary of the Oxford Movement, writing in the *Christian Observer* in 1844, has the following to say about the relationship of the Tractarians with monasticism:

> The key-stone of the Tractarian fabric is the monastic system. . . . But it behoves those who regard the signs of the times, to mark the insidious efforts which are in progress for introducing into the Anglican Church monastic institutions, constrained clerical celibacy, and the Popish confessional; three of the most prolific sources of evil and wickedness which the annals of man's fallen nature have furnished from the Fall to the Deluge, and from the Deluge to the present moment. . . . [B]inding the clergy to it [i.e., celibacy], and shutting up hundreds and thousands of men and women for life in nunneries and monasteries, has led to more depravity than any device of the most studied licentiousness. . . .

31. Faught, *Oxford Movement*, ix.
32. Cox, "Newman, Littlemore, and a Tractarian Attempt at Community," 344.
33. Kenyon, "Social Aspect of the Catholic Revival," 387.

Reforming the Monastery

> But some of the precursors in the new start of Tractarianism have freely spoken their minds, declaring that England can never be a religious nation till we have an unmarried priesthood, monastic institutions, and auricular confession. . . . Monachism, male and female,—we cannot iterate it too often—is the basis of the whole [Tractarian] system.[34]

Though this author is clearly an anti-Tractarian, his assessment seems to be historically accurate, as we will see below.

Though the most well-known member of the Oxford Movement was John Henry Newman, it would be best to begin with the aforementioned John Keble. Son of an Anglican priest, Keble matriculated at Corpus Christi College, Oxford in 1807, gaining double first-class honors four years later. The following year he won prizes for both his Latin and English essays and was appointed to a fellowship at Oriel College, Oxford, becoming a college tutor in 1817. In addition, Keble was ordained a priest and given charge of two village churches in the Oxford area. In 1827, Keble published *The Christian Year*, a collection of poetry organized around the liturgical calendar that became one of the best sellers of the nineteenth century, going through ninety-five editions during Keble's own lifetime. The success of *The Christian Year* gained Keble a nomination to the Oxford chair of poetry in 1821, which he declined. Instead, Keble left Oxford for parish life in 1823. However, in 1831, Keble accepted election as professor of poetry at Oxford University, a non-resident post that he held for ten years. Keble's greatest contributions to the Oxford Movement are his authorship of nine of the "Tracts for the Times" and his joint editorship, with John Henry Newman and Edward Pusey, of the "Library of the Fathers." Though Keble himself married in 1835, he was an advocate of the reestablishment of monasticism in the Church of England. In a letter to Newman dated March 3, 1844, Keble expresses to Newman his reserve that some of the Tractarians are advocates for English translations of Roman Catholic devotional texts, something that Keble is against. Instead, Keble writes,

> For my own part, until I could be convinced that this Church [of England] has no authority, I seem to see my way clearly thus far, that I ought to lay myself out upon those additions to her system and ritual which I am *sure* are in Antiquity, such as Monasticism,

---

34. "Romanist Saints and Tractarian Movements," 731–33 and 742.

Prayers for the Dead, etc., rather than upon those which by consent of all parties were not developed till afterwards.[35]

Thus, for Keble, monasticism is an ancient institution and should be reinstituted into the Church of England. For him, the presence of monasticism in the Christian church is not some novel addition of the later centuries, but the practice of the earliest centuries and thus worthy of inclusion in church life. Such sentiment is echoed in the writings of one of Keble's favorite contemporary poets, William Wordsworth. Wordsworth speaks approvingly of monasticism in several of this poetical works. In his *Ecclesiastical Sonnets*, published in 1822, he recounts in poetic form the history of the Christian church in England. Coming to the late medieval period, Wordsworth acknowledges that late medieval monasticism lacked its earlier vitality, going so far as to say that "Venus sits disguisèd like a Nun,— / While Bacchus, [is] clothed in semblance of a Friar."[36] Yet, when walking among the ruins of an abandoned abbey, he writes affirmingly of the place of monasticism in English church life, saying that Henry VIII and his assistants who dissolved the monasteries during the Reformation need to be forgiven:

> Monastic Domes! following my downward way,
> Untouched by due regret I marked your fall!
> Now, ruin, beauty, ancient stillness, all
> Dispose to judgments temperate as we lay
> On our past selves in life's declining day:
> For as, by discipline of Time made wise,
> We learn to tolerate the infirmities
> And faults of others, gently as he may,
> So with our own the mild Instructor deals,
> Teaching us to forget them or forgive.
> Perversely curious, then, for hidden ill
> Why should we break Time's charitable seals?
> Once ye were holy, ye are holy still;
> Your spirit freely let me drink, and live![37]

Elsewhere, he speaks very favorably of the good that the monasteries serve in relationship to humanity. In the summer of 1833, Wordsworth

---

35. Newman, *Correspondence of John Henry Newman*, 308. Italics in the original.
36. Sonnet XX, "Monastic Voluptuousness," in *Ecclesiastical Sonnets*, Part II.
37. Sonnet XXXV, "Old Abbeys," in ibid.

Reforming the Monastery

undertook a tour of England, writing the poem "Stanzas Suggested in a Steam-boat off St. Bees' Heads, on the Coast of Cumberland." St. Bees was an early monastic site, first inhabited in the mid-seventh century by Bega, a holy woman from Ireland. In time a small monastery was constructed, and after the Norman conquest of England, in 1066, Benedictine monks inhabited the monastery. Regarding their benevolent behavior to non-monastics, Wordsworth writes,

> There were the naked clothed, the hungry fed;
> And Charity extendeth to the dead
> Her intercessions made for the soul's rest
> Of tardy Penitents; or for the best
> Among the good (when love might else have slept,
> Sickened, or died) in pious memory kept:
> Thanks to the austere and simple Devotees,
> Who, to that service bound by veniel fees,
> Kept watch before the altars of St Bees.[38]

It is clear, then, that Wordsworth thought highly enough of monasticism to lament the closure of monastic houses during the Reformation as well as to say that monasteries assisted the physical and spiritual needs of individuals. It also goes without saying that the remains of the dissolved monasteries always impressed Wordsworth, since they were idyllic natural sites, especially the remains of Tintern Abbey on the River Wye. It was at Tintern Abbey, on July 13, 1798, that Wordsworth penned the following lines:

> ... Therefore am I still
> A lover of the meadows and the woods,
> And mountains; and of all that we behold
> From this green earth; of all the mighty world
> Of eye and ear, both what they half-create,
> And what perceive; well pleased to recognize
> In nature and the language of the sense,
> The anchor of my purest thoughts, the nurse,
> The guide, the guardian of my heart, and soul
> Of all my moral being.[39]

---

38. Wordsworth, *Complete Poetical Works of William Wordsworth*. The full text of "Saint Bees' Heads" is available online; see http://www.bartleby.com/145/ww815.html.

39. "Lines, Composed a Few Miles above Tintern Abbey," lines 103–11. The complete

Like Wordsworth, it was also a visit to Tintern Abbey that caused Keble to reflect further on the monastic life. In July 1825, Keble visited Tintern with Richard Hurrell Froude (d. 1836), another of the early and important Tractarians. In a letter to his father the following month, Froude describes the visit, writing that he and Keble made "a vow that if we died worth £100,000 we [would] leave it to repair the building & endow a choire [sic] & chapter but we [could] not agree about the statutes."[40] Their vow of endowing a choir and chapter shows that both Keble and Froude were open to the reestablishment of monasticism in England. In fact, Froude's very lifestyle shows that in many ways he was himself already living monastically.

Froude was born in 1803, the son of a priest of the Church of England. In 1821, he went to Oriel College, Oxford, where he came under the tutorship and spiritual influence of John Keble, who taught Froude that moral rightness was more valuable than mental rigorism. Following his studies, Froude was elected to a fellowship at Oriel in 1826 and ordained an Anglican priest in 1829. At about this same time, Froude underwent some form of religious crisis—the nature of which has remained a mystery—resulting in a lifestyle of extreme self-denial and scrutiny. The extent of his personal asceticism only came to light after his death with the publication of his *Remains*. Among the men of the Oxford Movement, Froude was the first champion of celibacy and other catholic ideals. Due to tuberculosis, Froude spent time traveling in the Mediterranean and serving the bishop in Barbados. He returned to England and died in February 1836. His *Remains* were edited and published by Keble and John Henry Newman in 1838, igniting a firestorm around the Oxford Movement. In the *Remains*, Froude's hatred of the Protestant Reformation and his reverence for the church's sacramental tradition comes to light, as does his own personal ascetic disciplines: "I use self-denial because I believe it the way to make the most out of our pleasures."[41] Froude himself connects his lifestyle with monasticism when, in October 1826, he writes,

> I have been coming to a resolution that, as soon as I am out of reach of observation, I will begin a sort of monastic austere life, and do my best to chastise myself before the Lord. That I will attend chapel regularly, eat little and plainly, drink as little wine as

---

text of "Tintern Abbey" is available online; see http://www.bartleby.com/145/ww138.html.

40. Quoted in Gelpi, "John Keble and Hurrell Froude in Pastoral Dialogue," 8.
41. Froude, *Remains*, 1:40. Hereafter cited parenthetically by page number.

Reforming the Monastery

> I can consistently with the forms of society: keep the fasts of the Church as much as I can without ostentation: continue to get up at six in the winter: abstain from all unnecessary expenses in every thing: give all the money I can save in charity, or for the adorning of religion.... I will avoid society as much as I can.... I will avoid all conversation on serious subjects ... and content myself with exercising dominion over my own mind, without trying to influence others. (25–26)

Elsewhere in the *Remains*, Froude not only further reveals his own self-denying practices ("slept on the floor"), but is more explicit about refounding monastic houses in England: "It has lately come into my head the present state of things in England makes an opening for reviving the monastic system" (322). However, as Barbara Gelpi shows, Froude's vision of a reestablished monasticism would look like and be characterized by historical monasticism—that is, single men and women under a vow of celibacy living together in a monastery, engaging in acts of self-denial, but all done for the good and betterment of the catholic Church of England. Keble, on the other hand, envisioned that a restored Anglican monasticism would resemble the Little Gidding experiment of Nicholas Ferrar, discussed previously. This likely accounts for why Keble and Froude could "not agree about the statutes" for a reestablished monasticism on their visit to the ruins of Tintern Abbey. In his poem for the first Sunday in Easter, "The Restless Pastor reproved," from *The Christian Year*, Keble speaks of his parsonage at Southrop, where he is curate, as a hermit's cell: "I thought it scorn with Thee to dwell, / A Hermit in a silent cell." The cause of this eremitical isolation is that Keble has fallen in love with a woman named Cornelia, who declined his offer of marriage. Though this event tempts Keble to "shun [his] daily task, / And hide [himself] for calm," he instead comes to see that "round each pure domestic shrine / Bright flowers of Eden bloom and twine; / Our hearths are altars all." In Keble's thought, monasticism was to be centered on the domestic sphere of married couples, children, and single persons all working and praying together. For Froude, the monastery would be the mediator between the monk and God, whereas for Keble, there was no need for such mediation, since one had access to God in the midst of daily activity and domestic life. It would be Froude's, as opposed to Keble's, ideas on monasticism that would come to characterize the larger Oxford Movement. With John Henry Newman and Edward Pusey, monasticism would come again to the Church of England.

John Henry Newman

John Henry Newman (d. 1890) is the most well-known and frequently studied of the Tractarians. Born in 1801 in London, Newman entered Trinity College, Oxford in 1817, obtaining a degree in classics in 1820. Elected to a fellowship at Oriel College in 1822, Newman, like Keble and Froude, was ordained an Anglican priest. After Keble preached his "National Apostasy" sermon, Newman became a driving force of the Oxford Movement. Fascinated with the early Christian fathers and the catholicity of the Church of England, Newman was the originator of the "Tracts for the Times," personally writing about one-third of the tracts. By the summer of 1839, Newman doubted the possibility of remaining an Anglican, given that he was more and more intellectually convinced of the truthfulness of the theological claims of the Roman Catholic Church. (Newman finally converted to Catholicism in October 1845.) At the same time, Newman was distraught at the number of young Anglicans who were converting to Roman Catholicism, believing that the Anglican church needed to provide the means whereby these young men could pursue the kinds of the spiritual lives that they were finding attractive in the Roman Catholic Church, including monasticism:

> I considered that to make the *Via Media* [i.e., Anglicanism] concrete and substantive, it must be much more than it was in outline; that the Anglican Church must have a ceremonial, a ritual, and a fulness of doctrine and devotion, which it had not at present, if it were to compete with the Roman Church with any prospect of success. Such additions would not remove it from its proper basis, but would merely strengthen and beautify it: such, for instance, would be confraternities, particular devotions, reverence for the Blessed Virgin, prayers for the dead, beautiful churches, munificent offerings to them and in them, monastic houses, and many other observances and institutions, which I used to say belonged to us as much as to Rome, though Rome had appropriated them and boasted of them, by reason of our having let them slip from us.[42]

Similarly, in a letter to his former student Thomas Mozley, he writes, "I should not be surprised to see conversions to Romanism some where or other. I think the women will be going, unless nunneries are soon held out

---

42. Newman, *Apologia pro sua vita*, 166–67.

to them *in* our Church."⁴³ Newman expresses the same fear about Anglican men: "I am almost in despair of keeping men together. The only possible way is a monastery. Men want an outlet for their devotional and penitential feelings—and if we do not grant it, to a dead certainty they will go where they can find it. This is the beginning and the end of the matter."⁴⁴ By the summer of 1841, Newman appears to have been intellectually convinced of the truthfulness of Roman Catholicism. In February 1842, he moved permanently to Littlemore, a small village outside of Oxford, to put into practice a scheme that he had developed two years prior. In his diary, on March 17, 1840, Newman wrote a memorandum titled "Reasons for living at Littlemore," giving as his third reason, "I hope for a *Monastic* house." On the same day Newman wrote to S. F. Wood, saying that he is "not without hope of setting up some day a real Monastery here [at Littlemore], and coming up myself to it, though I do not wish it to be talked about." Two days later, Newman received a letter from friend and fellow Tractarian, Edward Pusey. Pusey writes that he thinks Newman's desire to start a monastery at Littlemore is "valid" and that "it would be a great relief to have a *monē* in our Church, any ways, and you seem just the person to form one." By May, Newman had purchased the necessary land and wrote to his sister Jemima Mozley, "in due time [I] shall erect a Monastic House upon it."⁴⁵ In additional letters of 1840, Newman reveals his plan to others, referring to Littlemore as the site of a future "coenobitium" and "Abbey." By moving to Littlemore in 1842, Newman was clearly ready to institute his plans, creating "a departure platform for the revival of religious communities in the Church of England and in Anglicanism generally."⁴⁶

Newman's earliest printed words of favoritism towards monasticism were penned in 1835, though he had written about monasticism as early as 1829, in a poem titled "Monks." In this poem, Newman says that the monastic practices of vigils, fasting, and penance are "soul-ennobling" and that the monastic habit "fits [him] well." Six years later, in an anonymous article in the *British Magazine* titled "Letters on the Church of the Fathers," Newman writes that the "Monastic System" "has undoubtedly some especial [sic] in the providential conduct of our dispensation." He continues,

---

43. Newman, *Letters and Diaries*, 7:192.
44. Ibid., 8:410.
45. Ibid., 7:263, 266–67, and 334.
46. Cox, "Newman, Littlemore, and a Tractarian Attempt at Community," 343.

> I confess I regard the monastic life as holding a real place in the dispensation of the gospel. . . . Certainly it is as accordant with Scripture that a Christian should live in prayer and fasting, poverty and almsgiving, as that he should pass all his best days in making money, gain a patent of peerage, and found a family. It is not more culpable, *in the nature of things*, for a given individual to take a vow of celibacy, than to take a vow in marriage.[47]

Newman's main argument here is simple: just as it is natural for a married, family man to pray, fast, and give, so it is not against the gospel for a non-married man to do the same. As well, just as it is "in the nature of things" to make a vow of marriage, so it is not against nature to make a vow of celibacy. In the following year, also in the *British Magazine*, Newman makes a different argument. Here, he makes two suggestions: 1) those Anglicans who are especially devoted to Christ and the church need a means for living a more intentional spiritual life; and 2) parochial clergy are too busy to care adequately for all of those under their pastoral care. Cast as a dialogue between Newman and two friends, "Home Thoughts Abroad" says the following concerning monasticism:

> Clergymen at present are subject to the painful experience of losing the more religious portion of their flock. . . . They desire to be stricter than the mass of churchmen, and the church gives them no means. . . . [Religious Institutions] are imperatively called for to stop the progress of dissent: indeed, I conceive you necessarily must have dissent or monachism in a Christian country: so make your choice. The more religious [person] will demand some stricter religion than that of the generality of men . . . [or] you drive her to the dissenters: and why? All because the Religious Life, though sanctioned by the apostles and illustrated by the early saints, has before now given scope to moroseness, tyranny, and presumption. . . . I confess my hopes do not extend beyond the vision of the rise of this Religious Life among us. . . . Till then, I scarcely expect that anything will be devised of a nature to meet the peculiar evils existing in a densely peopled city . . . [for] great towns will never be evangelized merely by the parochial system. They are beyond the sphere of the parish priest, burdened as he is with the endearments and anxieties of a family, and the secular restraints and engagements of the establishment. . . . I think that Religious

---

47. Newman, "Letters on the Church of the Fathers," 663. Italics in the original.

> Institutions, over and above their intrinsic recommendations, are the legitimate instruments of working upon a populace.[48]

As well as in popular publications, Newman continued to talk to his correspondents about monasticism. For example, in a letter to Edward Pusey dated to January 12, 1836, Newman insists that early monasticism was not an institution of gloom, but rather one that had more of a striving after perfection in it, rather than merely a focus on penance. Several months later, when writing to Hugh Rose, Newman speaks of those practices that he believes the Church of England should have retained at the Reformation so as not to give up her birthright to the Roman Catholic Church. Newman suggests that should there be a "revolution" in the Anglican church resulting from the Oxford Movement, he "could just *fancy* a state of things in which a *novelty* in the Reformation Church, such as the rise of Monastic bodies, would be expedient—and if so, it is not harm to talk of it."[49] As seen above, the closer Newman got to converting to Roman Catholicism, the more he envisioned the need for Anglican monasticism.

In the *British Critic* of April 1842, Newman challenges comments made by John Davison, former fellow of Oriel College, Oxford, that appeared in Davison's, *Remains and Occasional Publications* of 1840. In short, Davison alleges that monks and nuns, by their very cloistered and contemplative vocation, are not engaged in the "active part" of "Christian charity," which is love of God *and* love of neighbor. Newman responds by insisting that, historically, monks and nuns were engaged in works of "active and self-denying charity," such as service in hospitals, schools, and orphanages. As well, "from the first the monastic bodies have been an instrument in the hands of Providence for the maintenance of orthodoxy" and "they were, as we all know, the preservers of ancient literature." Having demonstrated that this contention of Davison's was incorrect, Newman concludes by insisting that Davison is also incorrect in asserting "that monachism is inconsistent with our Lord's precepts." Newman responds,

> Now let us take the monastic rule, not as practised by those who lived in community, but even as carried out into its extreme by hermits, anchorites, fathers of the desert, and the like: are there no commands, as, for instance, concerning poverty and humility, which, taken in their first and obvious meaning, such a life literally and strikingly fulfils? We are not at all saying or dreaming, of

---

48. Newman, "Home Thoughts Abroad," 365–69.
49. Newman, *Letters and Diaries*, 5:302–3. Italics in the original.

course not, that all our Lord's precepts must be taken in the letter, yet it is better to observe them in the letter, than not to observe them at all. Now it is pretty clear that society, as at present constituted, does not keep the commands in question either in letter or spirit; also it seems to us clear, that whether a literal observance of them be necessary or not, monastic institutions do, of all others, most accurately and comprehensively fulfil the code of Gospel commandments, whether those which the present age does not fulfil, or those which it does.[50]

Also in 1842, volume seven of Newman's *Parochial and Plain Sermons* was published. In a sermon titled "Temporal Advantages," Newman speaks of how those within the earliest Christian communities sold all they had to give alms, washed one another's feet, and had all things in common. Furthermore, these early Christians formed themselves "into communities for prayer and praise, for labour and study, for the care of the poor, for mutual edification, and preparation for Christ." In fact, as soon as the world professed itself to be Christian, monks entered the church and "from that time to this, never has the union of the Church with the State prospered, but when the Church was in union also with the hermitage and the cell."[51] The following year, in 1843, Newman preached another sermon, titled "The Apostolical Christian," in which he returned to the theme of his *British Critic* article against John Davison—that is, that "the humble monk, and the holy nun, and other regulars" were "Christians after the very pattern given us in Scripture." Newman is led to this conclusion because he sees that monastics are the only Christians who "give up home and friends, wealth and ease, good name and liberty of will, for the kingdom of heaven." In fact, these monks and nuns are where one should look if one is seeking a modern-day Apostle Paul or Peter, or John the disciple, or Mary. For it is monastics who have made Christ "their all-sufficient, everlasting portion," though "those great surrenders which Scripture speaks of, are not incumbent on all Christians."[52] In a similar vein, also in 1843, in the sermon, "Indulgence in Religious Privileges," Newman speaks again on the institution of monasticism:

> I am not denying that there are certain individuals raised up from time to time to a still more self-denying life, and who have a

---

50. Newman, "John Davison," 414–18.
51. Newman, "Temporal Advantages," 69–70.
52. Newman, "Apostolical Christian," 290–92.

> corresponding measure of divine consolations. As some men are Apostles, others Confessors and Martyrs, as Missionaries in heathen countries may be called to give up all for Christ; so there are doubtless those, living in peaceable times and among their brethren, who acknowledge a call to give up every thing whatever for the sake of the Gospel, and in order to be perfect; and to become as homeless and as shelterless, and as resourceless and as solitary, as the holy Baptist in the wilderness: but extraordinary cases are not for our imitation, and it is as great a fault to act without a call as to refuse to act upon one.[53]

From these texts, it is clear that Newman saw monasticism as both warranted by the Bible—since it was merely the outgrowth of the Scriptures call to perfection—and a vocation to which some, but not all, are called. Monasticism was a special vocation for those called to austerity and self-denial, but despite its particularity, it was a call of God nonetheless, and therefore the institution needed to be present in the church of Jesus Christ, including the Church of England.

By 1845, Newman knew that he would not remain an Anglican and was growing exhausted by the consistent attacks being made on the Tractarians, including their views of monasticism. As early as 1834, Joseph Blanco White, a former Roman Catholic priest who converted to Anglicanism, wrote that Keble and Newman's reasoning regarding monasticism was an *argumentum ad absurdum*. He writes,

> It is curious . . . that if we admit the principle that Christian piety consists in devotional *practices*, there is no sound reason to object to Monachism. . . . Still more desirable would it be to have Monasteries, where Christians should pass their lives in singing psalms, in meditation, in pious reading—to which if they added preaching, and visiting the poor and sick, and fasting, and some other means which their desire of keeping the body under would easily suggest—we should have Monasteries among Protestants, exactly upon the plan of the Popish Orders.—I conceive, however, that this precept would not deter my friends [Keble and Newman]. Nor do I indeed mean that there is any thing positively wrong in all this. My objection arises from the circumstance that it is *not Christianity*.[54]

---

53. Newman, "Indulgence in Religious Privileges," 124.
54. White, *Life of the Rev. Joseph Blanco White*, 2:34–35. Italics in the original.

For White, all Christians are to live pious lives characterized by incessant prayer, as commended by the Apostle Paul. Thus, "if Prayer must be incessant ... it cannot be *formal*—it cannot be *external*. It must consist chiefly in the *desire* of the heart. ... *Living by Faith* is not an occupation."[55] Therefore, monasticism must *not* be a desirable ecclesial institution. Ten years later, the *Lives of the English Saints*, which Newman edited, was being attacked for its positive portrayal of monasticism. Future prime minister of England William Gladstone wrote that he was offended by "the relative position assigned to the papal and episcopal authorities, with respect to the monastic establishment" in the *Lives*. The most scathing attack, however, came from the Anglican priest, John Crosthwaite, in his *Modern Hagiology*. Crosthwaite did not mince words, accusing Newman and the contributors of failing to "to throw any light on the history of our church." Instead, he insists the project is motivated by the Oxford Movement's agenda to make the Anglican church in England conform to Roman Catholicism: "The character, then, of this new work, the *Lives of the English Saints*, is decidedly, and on many points, extravagantly Romish. It is, in fact, Popish." Crosthwaite quickly notices the pro-monastic stance of the work, writing, "the reader will be prepared to find Monasticism forming one of the main features of the system they are written to recommend. In truth, a very large portion of the series is occupied with this subject alone."[56] By the time Crosthwaite and others were done attacking the *Lives*, Newman was already a Roman Catholic. It would fall to the last major personality of the Oxford Movement to help establish Anglican monasticism institutionally.

Edward Pusey

Edward Pusey was born on August 22, 1800. He entered Christ Church, Oxford in January 1819 and obtained an Oriel College fellowship in 1823. After studying in Germany, Pusey was ordained an Anglican priest and awarded Oxford University's Regius professorship of Hebrew in 1828. Pusey's fellowship at Oriel introduced him to the other Oriel men responsible for the Oxford Movement—Keble, Froude, and Newman. Like Keble, Pusey remained a lifelong Anglican. Unlike Keble, however, Pusey was the only Tractarian who remained both an Anglican and in Oxford. Thus, by default and reluctantly, he was the movement's main spokesperson by 1845.

---

55. Ibid., 35. Italics in the original.
56. Crosthwaite, *Modern Hagiology*, 1:4 and 20.

Reforming the Monastery

Pusey's support of the reestablishment of monasticism in the Church of England is found primarily in the letters and entries published in volume three of Henry Liddon's *Life of Edward Bouverie Pusey* under the title "Early Days of Anglican Sisterhoods." As early as December 1839, Pusey wrote to John Keble,

> N[ewman] and I have separately come to think it necessary to have some "Sœurs de Charité" [Sisters of Charity] in the Anglo-Catholic [Church]. He is going to have an article on it in the *B[ritish] C[ritic]*. If no one else writes it, he will do it himself. I have named it since to very different sorts of persons, and all are taken with it exceedingly, (except B. H[arrison], who (as Archbishop's Chaplain) is half afraid of it,) and think that there would be numbers of people who are yearning to be employed that way. My notion was that it might begin by regular employment as nurses, in hospitals and lunatic asylums.

In the same month, he also wrote, in terms echoing his letter to Keble, to a priest in Leeds that he wants "very much to have one or more societies of 'Sœurs de la Charité' formed . . . [to] be employed in hospitals, lunatic asylums, prisons, among the females."[57] In March 1840, as quoted above, he responded to a letter from Newman affirming that Newman was the right person for founding a monastery at Littlemore. This should not be read as only a word of personal support for Newman, but also a word of support for monasteries as is also evidenced in Newman's letter to J. H. Bowden, where he reveals that, like himself, "Pusey is at present very eager about setting up Sisters of Mercy. I feel sure that such institutions are the only means of saving some of our best members from Roman Catholics." During this same time, Pusey was collecting rules from Roman Catholic religious houses in Paris so as to begin drawing up a set of rules for an Anglican sisterhood. Also, he visited Roman Catholic religious houses in Ireland in an attempt to learn firsthand about monasticism. Upon returning, he wrote to the Reverend E. Churton, "As to monasticism, I do not go further than Archbishop Leighton in what he says about 'retreats for men of —— and mortified tempers,' which he regrets were lost at the Reformation. I have long strongly thought that we needed something of this sort; it is not Romanist but primitive."[58] The following year, Pusey published a letter addressed to the archbishop of Canterbury in which he sought to defend

---

57. Liddon, *Life of Edward Bouverie Pusey*, 3:5–6.
58. Ibid., 2:271.

the Tractarians against their detractors. In this letter Pusey admits that the Roman Catholic Church "has, in her Monastic institutions, a refuge from the weariness and vanities of the world and a means of higher perfection to individuals, which many sigh after, and which might be revived in a primitive form, but which as yet we have not" in the Church of England.[59] In spite of this consistent exchange of ideas regarding the reinstitution of monasticism in the Church of England, its actual reestablishment was much more subdued than expected.

Though Pusey's own daughter, Lucy, had expressed an interest from a young age to become a religious sister, it was another woman who was first led to take religious vows. Marion Hughes was born on January 14, 1817, the daughter of a priest. Having heard Newman preach and having read his *Church of the Fathers*, Hughes came to know Pusey through the priest Charles Seager, a friend of Pusey, and Thomas Chamberlain, vicar of St. Thomas' Church, Oxford and Hughes's cousin. While reading Newman, Hughes had been particularly impressed by one passage:

> And if women have themselves lost so much by the present state of things, what has been the loss of the poor, sick, and aged, to whose service they might consecrate the life which they refuse to shackle by the marriage vow? What has been the loss of the ignorant, sinful, and miserable among whom they only can move without indignity who bear a religious character upon them; for whom they only can intercede or excert themselves who have taken leave of earthly hopes and fears; who are secured by their holy resolve from the admiring eye or persuasive tongue; and can address themselves to the one heavenly duty to which they have set themselves with singleness of mind?[60]

Despite a lack of monastic institutions, Hughes took the traditional monastic vows of poverty, chastity, and obedience before Pusey at the home of Seager on Trinity Sunday—that is, June 6, 1841. After taking her vows, she went to St. Mary's Church, Oxford, where she received communion from Newman, who was aware that she had just taken vows. Kneeling beside her at Holy Communion was Pusey's daughter, Lucy, who was receiving her first communion. Hughes's entry in her diary that evening is worth quoting:

> This day Trinity Sunday, 1841, was I enrolled one of Christ's Virgins, espoused to Him and made His handmaid and may He of

---

59. Ibid., 3:12.
60. Russell, *Household of Faith*, 56–57.

Reforming the Monastery

> His infinite mercy grant that I may ever strive to please Him, and to keep myself from the world though still in it, and should it be most mercifully granted that an opportunity may be given me to separate myself entirely from it, make me to rejoice in the means of taking the burden of His cross more closely to myself.[61]

Because of Hughes's family obligations, she was unable to immediately found an institution. However, she did travel with Seager and his wife to Normandy in the months after taking her vow, where she visited different Roman Catholic communities of nuns and studied their rules and constitutions. Ten years later, in 1851, she was able to finally establish the community of The Society of the Holy and Undivided Trinity in Oxford. In the meantime, Pusey continued to push for the founding of an Anglican sisterhood. In 1843, there appears to have been a discussion of starting a community in Bisley: "I agree with you that B[isley] would be a good place for a *monē* . . . for a few young women to live together in one house for the purposes of devotion and charity."[62] As well, in February 1843, Pusey wrote to Marion Hughes that though it was taking time to set up the first Anglican sisterhood, there was no doubt that individuals were being prepared for the task. Pusey writes,

> A longing for a life more given up to devotion and charity is being put into the minds of persons of both sexes. I have heard of much of this sort since I last saw you. The time is not lost, but rather gained, which passes before any formal institution is made. It is too great a work to be brought about readily and yet solidly. It might easily degenerate. The difficulties which people have to go through before they enter upon it are a means of disciplining them to enter upon it aright; and they, meantime, may be disciplining themselves by learning to give up more readily their own wills, bearing contradiction cheerfully, as well as growing continually in the grace and love and fear of God. The great dangers in beginning any such institution would be, that people would not be sufficiently ready to give up their own ways (each wishing to do good in their own), or not have command of temper, so as to bear the ways of those who might be strangers to them, or excited and wayward; or, again, others with a general notion of wishing to devote themselves to God's service, might still not have a standard sufficiently high. I doubt not, then, that while such institutions are for the time withheld, people are being prepared both to enter

---

61. Quoted in Allchin, *Silent Rebellion*, 59.
62. Ibid., 61.

them in a deeper spirit, and to welcome them more gratefully. Yet there must be continued prayer for them.[63]

Pusey was right, for it was in 1845 that the Park Village Community would finally reintroduce organized monasticism into the English church.

As mentioned previously, it was expected that Lucy Pusey would one day enter the religious life, perhaps even becoming the first superior of a monastic institution. This was not to be the case, however, given that Lucy died on April 22, 1844. Yet, on the day of her funeral, two letters addressed to Pusey were written. The first letter, from T. D. Acland, informed Pusey that two meetings had been held in London discussing the possibility of establishing an Anglican women's community. At the one meeting, a letter from the bishop of London, Charles Blomfield, was read, in which the bishop spoke of having consulted with the archbishop of Canterbury and being now ready to entertain any mature thoughts regarding the reinstitution of monasticism in the Church of England. The other letter, from John Manners, apprised Pusey of the results of a meeting in London attended by those in favor of beginning a woman's community as a monument to the memory of the poet Robert Southey. The committee that met imposed two conditions. First, it should be located in a parish whose priest would welcome it and serve as its spiritual head. It was suggested that the parish of Christ Church, St. Pancras in London under the oversight of Rev. William Dodsworth would serve as its home. Second, the bishop of London must sanction the endeavor. In his letter to Pusey, Manners reports that it was important that a woman who could serve as a superior be found, since any future plans would have to include her ideas. The attendants were interested in knowing if Pusey knew anyone who could serve as a superior. The members of the meeting "had resolved to take preliminary steps for the establishment and permanent maintenance of a Sisterhood living under a religious Rule and engaged in some work of mercy such as

1. Visiting the poor or the sick in their own homes.
2. Visiting hospitals, workhouses, or prisons.
3. Feeding, clothing, and instructing destitute children.
4. Assisting in burying the dead."[64]

---

63. Liddon, *Life of Edward Bouverie Pusey*, 3:12.
64. Ibid., 13.

Pusey was unable to commend anyone to the committee, but that would soon change.

Jane Ellacombe was the daughter of Henry Thomas Ellacombe, a priest, graduate of Oriel College, and friend of Newman. In 1844, Fr. Ellacombe wrote to Pusey asking if there was some place where his daughter could function as a governess while giving her time over to living the religious life. Pusey was unable to recommend a place, but he took it upon himself to offer Fr. Ellacombe some advice, from one father to another. Pusey suggests that Ellacombe create space in his own home for his daughter to try her vocation among a daily routine of prayer and service to the poor. Pusey sensed that Jane was hearing a call to the religious life and that she simply needed a space in which to test the "steadfastness" of her call. Pusey then tells the elder Ellacombe about the plans afoot in London for the establishment of a religious house. Finally, the committee in London, failing to find a suitable candidate for superior, procured a property in London. On March 26, 1845, the Wednesday of Easter week, two sisters arrived to take up lodging in the new foundation: Jane Ellacombe and Mary Bruce. They were soon joined by a daughter of the bishop of Edinburgh, then by Emma Langston, chosen to serve as the superior, and soon thereafter, four more women joined the community. The future of the community, which took the name of the "Sisterhood of the Holy Cross," was not without controversy and difficulty. Pusey, who became the de facto head of the community, and Dodsworth, the head of the community as per the London committee's directions, were in conflict over the direction of the community. Several years after the founding, Pusey provided funds for the sisters to move to a permanent location, moving them out of the parish of Christ Church and into the parish of St. Mary. The future of the community as it stood at that time would be short-lived, given that the Park Village Sisterhood merged with the Devonport Sisters of Mercy in 1856.

Priscilla Lydia Sellon was born on March 21, 1821, the daughter of a Royal Navy officer and his first wife.[65] Raised in a large religious family, it was in 1848 that Sellon responded to an appeal placed in the church newspaper, *The Guardian*, by Henry Phillpotts, bishop of Exeter. In this letter, dated January 1, 1848, Phillpotts describes the population density of the city of Devonport, a suburb of Plymouth, in the southwest of England, and its desperate need for additional Christian workers to help reach the population who had only one parish church. Giving careful consider-

---

65. Much of the following is taken from Williams, *Priscilla Lydia Sellon*.

The Anglican Tradition

ation to this request, Sellon secured the approval of her father and Bishop Phillpotts. She then traveled to London to consult with family friends, the Chambers, and Pusey. Sellon arrived in Devonport in April 1848, where she spent several months ministering to neighbors and the many children that she encountered on the streets. By the summer, she was ill, having exhausted herself, and was forced to take a break. During this period of recovery, she was encouraged by Pusey and her father to found a sisterhood, which would ensure organization, growth, and stability of the work. Sellon was not unfamiliar with the reintroduction of monastic life into the Anglican Church, as she had visited the Park Village Sisterhood, likely in 1847. Receiving Bishop Phillpotts' blessing on the sisterhood, Sellon visited the Village Park community again. She returned to Davenport in October with the Chambers' daughter Catherine, opening a home for orphaned daughters of poor sailors.

The new home was dedicated by Bishop Phillpotts in October 1848, at which time he also gave his official sanction to the sisterhood, which adopted the name The Church of England Sisterhood of Mercy of Devonport and Plymouth. As Sellon and Chambers knelt before the bishop on October 27 to receive his blessing, they consecrated themselves to God, regarding this as their formal profession and consecration as Sisters of Mercy. According to their rule of life at the time, the women would spend six hours each day working among the poor, tending the sick, and visiting schools. By the end of 1848, three more women had joined Sellon and Chambers, bringing the number of sisters to five. One of these sisters, Sarah Terrot, transferred from the Park Village Sisterhood in London. The devotional and liturgical life of the sisters is laid out in a letter from Chambers to a prospective candidate, dated February 3, 1849. The sisters rose early in the morning for private devotions before eating breakfast together at 7:00 a.m. They then proceeded to the parish church for the 8:00 a.m. morning service. After morning service came work, with pauses at 9:00 a.m., noon, and 3:00 p.m. to engage in devotion and prayers in remembrance of the Passion of Jesus Christ. This was followed by attendance at the evening service in the parish church, followed by an hour of devotional reading and prayers at bedtime, which was said to be at 10:00 p.m. Sellon's fame did not escape the notice of the great poet William Wordsworth, who wrote "To Miss Sellon" on February 22, 1849:

> The vestal priestess of a Sisterhood,
> Who knew no self and whom the selfish scorn,

Reforming the Monastery

> She seeks a wilderness of weed and thorn,
> And undiverted from her blessed mood
> By keen reproach or blind ingratitude,
> A wreath she twines of blossoms lowly born—
> An amaranthine crown of flowers forlorn—
> And hangs her garland on the Holy Rood.
>
> Sister of Mercy! bravely hast thou won,
> From men who winnow charity from faith,
> The pharisaic sneer that treats as dross
> The works ordained by faith. Pursue thy path,
> Till, at the last, thou hear the voice, "Well done,
> Thou good and faithfull servant of the Cross."[66]

For all practical purposes, the community started off a great success and continued to flourish in spite of anti-monastic and anti-Tractarian sentiment from many in the Plymouth area and across England.

By 1852, the community was composed of three orders within the Sisterhood. The "Sisters of the Holy Communion" were engaged in active works of charity. The "Sisters of the Sacred Heart" were basically cloistered nuns who spent their time writing and creating church art, as well as engaging in private and corporate prayer. The "Sisters of Charity of the Holy Ghost" were a third order, composed of women who lived and worked at one of the houses of the Sisterhood, as well as associates who temporarily lived and worked in one of the houses. In October 1850, the community's first permanent house, known as St. Dunstan's Abbey, was started, though its full range of buildings was never completed. As mentioned above, in 1856 the Park Village community merged with the Devonport sisters, with Sellon installed as "abbess" of the two communities, who were renamed "The Congregation of Religious of the Society of the Most Holy Trinity." New statutes were drawn up the same year in order to more clearly define the three orders of the community. The first order was dedicated "to the Praise, Glory, and Adoration of . . . the First Person of the Coequal and Undivided Trinity" and was made up of the Sisters of Mercy, whose object was "to extend the kingdom of Christ by teaching the doctrines of the Catholic Religion, and devoting themselves to works of mercy under religious

---

66. Wordsworth, *Poetical Works of William Wordsworth*, 3:325.

discipline and apart from the world."[67] These sisters lived at St. Dunstan's Abbey, reciting all of the canonical hours while engaging in works of mercy and charity. The second order was dedicated to the Son of God and was comprised of cloistered nuns whose constitutions were based on Roman Catholic precedents. They were not allowed to leave the monastery except to attend church, spending their days in prayer, praying in particular "for the conversion of sinners throughout the world, and for a blessing on the labours of their Sisters of the two other Orders, that they might be the means of bringing many souls to the knowledge and love of God."[68] The third order was dedicated to the Holy Spirit and its sisters were aimed at "assuaging suffering in whatever form."[69]

In the following years, the number of sisters dwindled and many of the charitable activities of the sisters were given up in favor of a more contemplative vocation. Sellon, however, desired to maintain two of the society's works in particular: the care of orphans and the care of convalescent patients. To facilitate this work, a new house was built near Ascot with money left to Pusey by his mother. St. Dunstan's Abbey remained the mother house of the community, but Sellon herself lived most of the time at Ascot Priory. Significantly, the Society was the first Anglican sisterhood to take up mission work outside of England, when four of the sisters set up St. Andrew's Priory in Honolulu, Hawaii, in 1867. Despite these efforts, in 1868, the Society only numbered fourteen sisters of the first two orders. Upon the death of Sellon on November 20, 1876, it was discovered that the community was in a desperate financial situation. Pusey, appointed Warden of the community, and the new superior, Bertha Turnbull, decided to receive no more postulants in the first and third orders, effectively turning the community, originally founded as Sisters of Mercy, into a cloistered community that had oversight of two schools in Plymouth and an orphanage and convalescent home at Ascot. In 1906, St. Dunstan's Abbey was leased to another sisterhood and Ascot Priory became the only house of the Society. On February 12, 2004, the last sister of the Society died at Ascot Priory, bringing an end to Sellon's work.[70]

The history of Anglican communities of men is no less interesting than that of the women's communities. One example should suffice. On

67. Anson, *Call of the Cloister*, 269.
68. Ibid., 270.
69. Ibid.
70. See http://www.ascotpriory.org.uk/MotherCecilaPage.htm.

Reforming the Monastery

July 22, 1863, John Keble preached a sermon at St. Mary's Home in Wantage titled "Women Labouring in the Lord." In this sermon, Keble notes the important role that women played in the Bible, as well as in reintroducing the Church of England to monasticism. He then writes, "Why may we not hope that even within this generation Christian Brotherhoods as well as Sisterhoods of Mercy may be found taking their place in the work of Christ among us?"[71] Though it did take longer for men's communities to come into being, it happened nonetheless. In 1864–65, a priest named Simeon Wilberforce O'Neill published a serialized article in *The Ecclesiastic* titled "An Inquiry after the Secondary Causes of Success in Christian Missions." In his conclusion, he writes,

> These narratives seem to lead us irresistibly to the conclusion that monastic bodies have always been the most successful agents in the conversion of heathen nations. The missionaries have both had their training in the monasteries before entering upon their work, and also maintained the monastic character of their life when engaged in that work.... Seeing, therefore, that the need of religious houses of men is so great for the perfection of our Church and her success in propagating the Gospel, it has been resolved to form a monastic body of clergy and laymen under the spiritual direction of a most able guide. The rule of life will not be too lax to be efficient nor yet so severe as to be burdensome.... The aim and object of this society will be mission work both at home and abroad.... Any person who feels called by God to give himself to this work may have further particulars by applying to the writer of this paper.[72]

Soon after the article appeared, two men volunteered to serve as lay brothers in the envisioned community. Thereafter, two other men, Charles Grafton, an American clergyman, and his spiritual director, Oliver Prescott, were advised by Edward Pusey to get in touch with O'Neill. A meeting was held in London, with a second following in February 1865 that had Richard Meux Benson in attendance. By the end of this meeting, it was clear to those present that Benson and Grafton were both intent on living the kind of life described by O'Neill in his essay. At a third meeting, at which Pusey was present, it was decided that Benson would direct the start of the new community.

71. Keble, "Women Labouring in the Lord," 17.
72. O'Neill, "Inquiry after the Secondary Causes of Success in Christian Missions," 130–31.

Benson was an Oxford educated priest born in 1824. In 1850, he was appointed Vicar of Cowley, Oxford, where he ministered to the poor, dedicated himself to prayer, and felt a call to missionary work in India, though he had stayed in Oxford at the urging of his bishop. It was decided that the nascent community was to live at Benson's modest house in Cowley, so the need arose for them to gain episcopal approval for their endeavor. In July 1865, Benson wrote to Samuel Wilberforce, bishop of Oxford, describing the new community as a "Congregation of Priests and laymen, giving up the world, living by simple rule and devoting ourselves to prayer, study and mission work."[73] Their manner of life would involve week-long missions in any parish to which they were invited, ongoing mission work in London, a scholars house in Oxford for those desiring to live under a rule while studying at the university, a chapel in London to be used in outreach to the educated populace, foreign missions, and retreats. Bishop Wilberforce, after further discussions, blessed the new endeavor. Therefore, the community's birth is dated to August 1865, when Benson and Grafton took up residence together under a common rule of life. On December 27, 1866, Benson, Grafton, and O'Neill (author of the original call for a men's community) made their lifelong religious professions of celibacy, poverty, and obedience as mission priests of the Society of St. John the Evangelist. Soon thereafter, Benson compiled a rule for the community whose purpose was "to seek that sanctification to which God in His Mercy calls us, and in so doing to seek, as far as God may permit, to be instrumental in bringing others to be partakers of the same sanctification."[74]

The constitution of the community was to be priests professed under final vows, along with lay brothers who would have no vote or voice in the community's chapter. The novitiate would last for two years and no one would be allowed to make lifelong vows until the age of thirty. Those under thirty were only allowed to make vows lasting for one year, to be renewed annually. In a short time, the community grew and by 1883 there were missions in the United States, India, and South Africa. John Mackarness, bishop of Oxford, approved the Rule and Constitution of the "Cowley Fathers," as they were now known, on September 22, 1884. Having stepped down as superior in 1890, Benson died on January 14, 1915. The success of the Cowley Fathers should not only be measured in how quickly they spread outside of England, but in the fact that they continue in existence today. As

---

73. Quoted in Anson, *Call of the Cloister*, 77.
74. Ibid., 79.

Reforming the Monastery

it turns out, Benson's foundation, though born a good number of years after those of women's communities, has the distinction of being the longest lasting Anglican religious community founded since the Reformation. Though not without trouble, the monastic life that many had lamented as lost at the Reformation and desired to see again was finally restored in the Anglican Communion, where it continues today.

THREE
Karl Barth and Dietrich Bonhoeffer

KARL BARTH

Karl Barth was born on May 10, 1886, in Basel, Switzerland, to Fritz, a Reformed minister and university professor of New Testament and early church history at Bern, and his wife, Anna, a descendant of the Protestant reformer Heinrich Bullinger. In 1904, Barth began his university studies in Bern, followed by further studies at the universities of Berlin, Tübingen, and Marburg, where he adopted the liberal theological positions of Adolf von Harnack and Wilhelm Herrmann. Upon completion of his studies in 1909, he served for two years as a pastor in Geneva (preaching from the pulpit of John Calvin), moving to the small Swiss village of Safenwil in 1911. While in Safenwil, he came to reject the liberal theology that he received at university, finding it unsuited to address the problems of parish life and discordant with his own personal spiritual and theological journey. In 1919, he published his *Epistle to the Romans*, which, according to Eberhard Busch, "ushered in a new theological epoch. In it he called for a turning aside from anthropocentricity, arguing that God is always alien to all our religious and cultural thinking."[1] From 1921 to 1935, Barth taught theology at the universities of Göttingen, Münster, and Bonn, beginning during this time his *magnum opus*—the *Church Dogmatics* (which he continued working on until his death). In 1933, during the rise of National Socialism, Barth wrote *Theological Existence Today*, summoning the church to be obedient to God alone. By this he helped to found the Confessing Church of Ger-

1. Busch, "Barth, Karl," 209.

many (those church groups that refused the interference of the National Socialists into the state-run German Evangelical Church), which held the Synod of Barmen in May 1934 and issued the "Barmen Declaration" (with Barth as the primary author). Due to his opposition to National Socialism, Barth was dismissed from the University of Bonn, so he accepted a professorship at the University of Basel in Switzerland, teaching there until his retirement in 1962. In retirement, Barth was influential in ecumenical Christian circles, especially in 1966 when he traveled to the Vatican in Rome to talk with those involved in the Roman Catholic Church's Second Vatican Council. Barth died on December 10, 1968, leaving his *Church Dogmatics* unfinished.

It is not surprising that Barth, judged "the most important Protestant theologian since Schleiermacher" by John Webster, would be supportive of monasticism, given his familial connection to the Pietist movement (that is, those who emphasize a personal, individual conversion, on heartfelt union with Christ, and on the importance of the Scriptures as a guide in the spiritual life). As recounted by Eberhard Busch in *Karl Barth and the Pietists*, Barth's great-great-grandfather, Johann Burckhardt (d. 1820), was the founder of a Pietistic group called the Society of Christianity and was on familiar terms with the Herrnhutt community of Nicholas von Zinzendorf. The goal that the Society of Christianity, the German church historian L. von Rohden wrote in 1857, "set for itself was the preservation of the pure doctrine and a Christian way of life. The members were to strengthen each other in faith and confession; they joined for regular prayer, a conscientious observance of Sunday, the maintenance of household devotion, and strict discipline and self-examination." The Herrnhutt community had been founded in the 1720s as a Pietistic enclave where individuals were able to live in community with one another. Moreover, Burckhardt was the son-in-law of the great Basel Pietist Hieronymus Annoni, associate of Gerhard Tersteegen (d. 1769), who for most of his life lived some form of an intentional monastic life, whether as a hermit or in his "Brotherhood of Common Life." In two of his spiritual verses published in *The Spiritual Garden of Interior Souls*, Tersteegen praises the monastic life. In "The Happy Hermit," he writes that joy and freedom belong to the one "who lives alone with God." The hermit, "though in the world," is "inwardly on high." In "Contentment in the Cloister," Tersteegen claims that his presence in a cell demonstrates the depth of his soul. This well of solitary existence inebriates him so that he longs to remain there at all times. For Tersteegen, it is regretful that Protestant reformers so easily dismissed monasticism: "It is a known fact that many Protestant theologians have come to the conclusion that it would have been better if the monasteries had not been suppressed at the Reformation but merely reformed.... Indeed, I would say straight out that if the monasteries had been like those founded by St Teresa [of Ávila] at the time of the Reformation, no one could have suppressed them without grievously offending God."[2]

Barth's father, Fritz, was also influenced by the Pietistic heritage of Switzerland and Germany. In his book of 1913, *Christ Our Hope*, Fritz Barth speaks very highly of a Pietist named T. Beck, whom he credits with his conversion. For the elder Barth, Pietism has four strengths: "(1) the priority of life over doctrine; (2) its view of spiritual rebirth; (3) the close connection of justification to sanctification; and (4) the idea of the coming of the kingdom of God, both limiting and expanding the church as an institution."[3] Finally, the younger Barth was also educated in youth at a Pietistic school. Thus, in a letter to Charlotte Gelzer (widow of the Pietist Heinrich Gelzer) on October 30, 1963, Barth could write that he was "deeply indebted from the point of view of some of my ancestors, and then on the basis of my studies as well" to the Pietist tradition (286). Though critical of Pietism in his later theology, this stream of the Christian tradition influenced Barth and it certainly made its way into his early theology. For example, in his earliest published theological work, written during his pastorate in Safenwil, titled "Christian Faith and History," Barth says that true faith is "a developmental process in the life of the individual" encompassing an "individual liveliness" and an "actualization of heightened states of consciousness," that is, "'an inner experience' that as such is immediate, yet at the same time irrefutable and unprovable" (13). Putting it into Pietistic terms, Barth says that "faith is an experience of God" (13). This individualistic emphasis on one's own faith is a hallmark of Pietistic soteriology, so much so that Barth, to use the words of Busch, "thought he agreed with the *Pietists* in [his] understanding of faith" (15). This Pietistic influence is also evident in a sermon from August 18, 1907, where Barth says that Christians believe "what they themselves have experienced ... [for] the most inward and greatest truth is what takes place in our hearts" (15). Among the Pietists that Barth admired was the aforementioned Gerhard Tersteegen. In 1910, Barth gave a lecture

2. Zeller, "Protestant Attitude to Monasticism," 183.

3. Busch, *Karl Barth and the Pietists*, 12. Hereafter cited parenthetically by page number.

on Tersteegen, where Barth says that Tersteegen is "one of the greatest men we have, a prophet of *concentration* in life and thought, of *inwardness* of the soul and its redemption, of the *superiority* of God who made us and not we who made him." In Barth's understanding, Tersteegen's faith grew "not from confession to experience, but from experience to confession," which is "the way of self-denial" (17). Yet, Tersteegen's self-denial, Barth believed, went too far, becoming a denial of the world rather than a denial of the self. In the words of Busch,

> Tersteegen's path of self-denial was impressive to [Barth], but he found it problematic that Tersteegen confused *self*-denial with a denial of the *world*. In fact, Barth thought "even as good a Calvinist as Gerhard Tersteegen was in this respect fully Catholic. For him the world was only a deafening noise from which one must escape!" Barth sensed that Tersteegen put less emphasis on the "denial" and more on the "self" that has to be denied. For Barth the opposite was the case; self-denial, by objecting only to the "ego," to egotism, ruled out all attempts to take flight from the world. (19)

Yet, despite this critique, which would become more pronounced in his later works, it is important to see that Barth knew Pietism and affirmed its individualistic and self-denying nature, though not uncritical of certain aspects of the movement. Is it possible that this early influence remained with Barth throughout his theological career? Did the Pietistic emphasis on self-denial manifest itself in Barth's later writings? Eberhard Busch believes so and this may account for Barth's later positions on monasticism in imitation of his own favorite Pietist, Tersteegen.

Barth's greatest theological work is his fourteen-volume *Church Dogmatics*, left incomplete at his death. This series was an attempt to tackle all the themes of theological dogmatics and ethics from the perspective that Jesus Christ is the fulfillment of God's covenant with his people, reconciling them to himself and to one another so that they can grow in holiness. The proposed work was divided into five volumes: 1) the doctrine of the word of God; 2) the doctrine of God; 3) the doctrine of creation; 4) the doctrine of reconciliation (incomplete); and 5) the doctrine of redemption (not started). The volumes were then divided into parts and finally into chapters (see Figure 1). Much of Barth's theology of monasticism occurs in volume four, under the doctrine of reconciliation (see Figure 2). Before looking in detail, however, at volume four of the *Church Dogmatics*, it will be helpful to look to Barth's earliest comments on monasticism, in his book

Karl Barth and Dietrich Bonhoeffer

The Theology of Calvin from 1922, the lectures on ethics from 1928–29, and his brief comments in volume one, part two of the *Church Dogmatics*.

Barth accepted the call to become Professor of Reformed Theology at the University of Göttingen in 1921. In the summer of 1922, he lectured four hours a week on the theology of the great Genevan reformer of the sixteenth century John Calvin, with these lectures then published in the same year as *The Theology of Calvin*. His first comments regarding monasticism in this text come in a section where Barth is noting the common features between the Reformation and medieval era. Among a discussion of six common features, the first is "the problem of monasticism that was always present in the church from Benedict of Nursia by way of the Cluny reform to Francis of Assisi."[4] Barth's understanding of monasticism at this point in his career and where he sees it sharing common features with the Reformation is worth quoting at length:

> Originally we had here [in monasticism] a real protest of the first order against the theology of glory. . . . Initially monasticism questioned and even attacked a self-assured and worldly Christianity. It was an uplifted finger to remind people that we cannot have the kingdom of God so cheaply. The world took notice and caused the finger to drop. It made a place for asceticism. It offered this hard and dangerous function to the brave who were ready for it. It celebrated a new triumph by putting this possibility too, this highest level of human action, on the church's horizontal line. Thus the ascetics, though often with great pain . . . became protagonists of the triumphing world church instead of protesting against it. That does not alter the fact, however, that the Reformation was at least also an extension of the monastic line. The question of true penitence that brought the theology of the cross to the fore was a variation on a typically monastic question. Monasticism now mounted its most powerful offensive. With full seriousness and with no holding back it now broke out of the cloister and became a universal matter. It would now question the world, not as before from outside, but from inside, not in the form of the ascetic lifestyle of a few, but in that of a cross lifted up in the life of all. It achieved perhaps its greatest victory in the man in whom it finally went bankrupt [i.e., Martin Luther].[5]

Here we see Barth commending the institution of monasticism for standing up against the worldliness or the secularizing tendency of earliest

4. Barth, *Theology of John Calvin*, 50.
5. Ibid., 50–51.

Christianity. Monasticism created the space for those who were called to lead lives of radical asceticism and for helping the church keep its focus on the horizontal level of loving one's neighbor as well as on the vertical element of loving the Lord God with all one's heart, mind, and soul. In addition, Barth sees the Reformation as a widening of the institution of monasticism into the whole church (a sentiment that he shares with Martin Luther)! The Reformation was not a triumph over the institution of monasticism but a continuation of it. Would it be too much to say that Barth, at least in this context, approved of the institution of monasticism because it gave birth, so he says, to the Reformation itself? In the same work, Barth tempers, if just a little, his judgment on monasticism. Barth understands that the practice of asceticism, "the attempt to win freedom from the world," leads ultimately to "the attainment of the assessing and shaping and controlling of the world." For Barth, "this necessary link had brought two apparent antitheses, the papacy and monasticism, into alliance."[6] To Barth's mind, this is not a good marriage. As we will see below, Barth did not always remain so positive or laudatory about monasticism, but it would appear that as a young professor he found himself in agreement with the spirit of monasticism, if not with the institutional form itself.

In the summer and winter semester of 1928, while teaching at Münster, Barth lectured on ethics. These lectures were supplemented and delivered again in 1930–31 at Bonn. Though never published in his lifetime, these lectures were published in the original German in 1973 and 1978 and appeared in an English translation in 1981. Barth began the lectures with a very brief historical overview of the subject as a particular discipline within the field of theology. He says that there has not always been theological ethics, yet "the question of the goodness of human conduct has been raised and answered by theologians from the very first."[7] He affirms the supposition that "the author of the supposedly oldest Christian *ēthika* or collection of Christian rules of life was none other than the great theoretician and organizer of Eastern monasticism, Basil of Caesarea." Though Barth is not yet making any comment on monasticism proper, he is acknowledging that the oldest work of theological ethics is a set of monastic ascetical texts and rules written by Basil. To explain why the earliest theological ethical texts were monastic documents, Barth goes on to explain

---

6. Ibid., 127.
7. Barth, *Ethics*, 5. Hereafter cited parenthetically by page number.

Figure 1: Structure of Karl Barth's *Church Dogmatics*

Volume I: *The Doctrine of the Word of God*

I/1	I/2			
Ch. 1: Word of God as Criterion of Dogmatics	Ch. 3: Holy Scripture			
Ch. 2: Revelation of God	Ch. 4: Proclamation of the Church			
1932	1939			

Volume II: *The Doctrine of God*

II/1	II/2			
Ch. 5: Knowledge of God	Ch. 7: Election of God			
Ch. 6: Being of God	Ch. 8: Command of God			
1940	1942			

Volume III: *The Doctrine of Creation*

III/1	III/2	III/3	III/4	
Ch. 9: Work of Creation	Ch. 10: The Creature	Ch. 11: The Creator and His Creature	Ch. 12: Command of God the Creator	
1945	1948	1950	1951	

Volume IV: *The Doctrine of Reconciliation* (unfinished)

IV/1	IV/2	IV/3.1	IV/3.2	IV/4	
Ch. 13: Doctrine of Reconciliation	Ch. 15: Jesus Christ, the Servant as Lord	Ch. 16: Jesus Christ, the True Witness	Ch. 16: Jesus Christ, the True Witness (continued)	Fragment on Baptism	The Christian Life (posthumous fragment)
Ch. 14: Jesus Christ, the Lord as Servant					
1953	1955	1959	1960	1968	

Volume V: *The Doctrine of Redemption* (not started)

Source: Fred Sanders. Sanders is a colleague in the Torrey Honors Institute of Biola University.

**Figure 2: Structure of Karl Barth's *Doctrine of Reconciliation*
(*Church Dogmatics* Volume IV)**

Volume:	IV/1	IV/2	IV/3
Chapter:	14: Jesus Christ, the Lord as Servant	15: Jesus Christ, the Servant as Lord	16: Jesus Christ, the True Witness
	The Obedience of the Son of God (§59)	The Exaltation of the Son of Man (§64)	The Glory of the Mediator (§69)
Way:	The Way of the Son of God into the Far Country (§59.1)	The Homecoming of the Son of Man (§64.2)	The Light of Life (§69.2)
	The Judge Judged in Our Place (§59.2)	The Royal Man (§64.3)	Jesus is Victor! (§69.3)
Nature of Christ:	True God	True Man	True Witness
Office	Priest	King	Prophet
State	Humiliation	Exaltation	Both
Sin shown as:	Pride and Fall (§60)	Sloth and Misery (§65)	Falsehood and Condemnation (§70)
Grace as:	Justification (§61)	Sanctification (§66)	Vocation (§71)
Trinitarian appropriation:	Verdict of the Father (Yes and No judgment)	Direction of the Son (horizontal and vertical)	Promise of the Spirit (big and little hope)
Spirit's work in community:	Gathering (§62)	Upbuilding (§67)	Sending (§72)
Spirit's work in individual:	Awakening to Faith (§63)	Quickening in Love (§68)	Enlightening to Hope (§73)
Ethics (from IV/4):	Baptism as the Foundation of the Christian Life	The Lord's Prayer as the Fulfillment of the Christian Life	The Eucharist as the Renewal of the Christian Life
John 14:6	I am the Way	I am the Life	I am the Truth
1 Cor 1:30	Christ Became for Us Righteousness	And Sanctification	And Wisdom from God

Source: Fred Sanders

that the "presupposition on which an independent Christian ethics arose is obviously the concept of the possibility and reality of an evident human holiness, of a perfect Christian life which could be demanded from and realized by all Christians . . . and by the clergy and especially the monks"

(6). When discussing medieval Christianity, Barth lists the Rule of Benedict as a "well-known" ethical statement along with the *Imitation of Christ* of Thomas à Kempis. In a more critical tone, Barth notes that even in the vast theological project of Thomas Aquinas' *Summa theologica*, the "comprehensive and purely scientific account of ethics" found there "unambiguously has its basis in Aristotle and its crown and true scope in the religious life in the narrowest sense of the term, namely, the life of the clergyman and the monk" (6). It is clear in these lectures that Barth was not in favor of such a narrowly focused idea of ethics. Moreover, this hints at Barth's hesitations regarding the religious (i.e., monastic) life, something that he will flesh out in greater detail in the *Church Dogmatics*.

Elsewhere in the *Ethics*, however, Barth refers to "the Roman Catholic ideal of monasticism" as a kind of lifestyle "lying in a radical milieu" (470). His statement here is neither positive nor negative vis-à-vis monasticism, but occurs in the context of how some ethicists miss the nature of such movements. Similarly, in a section on conscience, Barth states that a "busy waiting for the Lord is what has obviously been the point... of the monasticism of the Roman Catholic Middle Ages to the extent—and it had other interests as well—that the development of the contemplative life is one of its characteristics" (489). Thus, at this point, circa 1930, Barth saw monasticism, at least in its Roman Catholic manifestations, as a radical form of life lived in an effort to direct one's conscience towards Christ. Yet, in the *Ethics*, such an emphasis can also be found in "the mysticism of all ages and types," in "the older Lutheranism of a Paul Gerhardt," in "the Eastern Church with its humility," and in Pietism. It is only in the *Church Dogmatics* that Barth gives greater comment to monasticism as an institution.

Writing volume one, part two of the *Church Dogmatics* less than ten years after delivering his ethics lectures in Münster, Barth largely repeats what he said in the lectures regarding the history of theological ethics:

> We can see both the suggested motifs in the increasingly independent ethical systems of Christian antiquity and the Middle Ages: the material motif, i.e., insight into the evident perfection of Christian character as developed in monastic life in the *Ēthika* of Basil of Caesarea, or the well-known rule of Benedict of Nursia, or the *Imitatio Christi* attributed to Thomas a Kempis; and the formal motif, i.e., the reaching back to a general or Aristotelian and Stoic anthropology in the *Moralia* of Gregory the Great.[8]

---

8. Barth, *Church Dogmatics* I/2, 783.

Reforming the Monastery

As in the *Ethics*, Barth is not making a statement about monasticism as an institution, but only as the earliest sources of a stated theological ethics. Finally, in 1955, however, Barth offered his most sustained reflection on the institution of monasticism proper in the *Church Dogmatics* volume four, part two, under a discussion on the reconciliatory work of Jesus Christ, the Son of Man. In particular, Barth is concerned in this section with the person reconciled with God in Jesus Christ, "the covenant man who faces the covenant God in the reconstitution and renewal of the covenant."[9] What this means for Barth is that we must not lose sight of the fact that humanity, specific men and women, were reconciled with God in Christ Jesus. Therefore, dogmatics must take seriously the fact that reconciliation is a movement from above to below (Jesus' incarnation), but also a move from below to above (humankind's response to Jesus' incarnation). This is a necessary discussion, says Barth, because theology needs "to attempt to understand the grace of God as the grace which is addressed to man and exalts and changes and renews him."[10] Yet, Barth is aware of the hazards of engaging in this project, believing that many theologies have made grave mistakes in this area. This is not a reason, believes Barth, to ignore the topic, but rather instead that he should embark on this inquiry fully aware of the hazards. He then lays out the fact that this opportunity is a "good reason to give to the Christian tendencies and movements which in this connexion [sic] are usually thought of in a predominantly or even exclusively critical way the cool and collected discussion which is their right."[11] One of these, in fact the first of these, is the institution of monasticism.

Barth begins with monasticism because in it he sees a movement that is particularly significant to the question of humankind's role or response to God's act of reconciling the world to himself, and because it consists in a "wealth and complexity of continually new forms" that have asserted themselves almost since the beginnings of the church. Furthermore, this is a productive area of discussion because the institution will continue into the future. Though Barth does not defend the sixteenth-century Reformers for rejecting monasticism, he is concerned that its reintroduction into "Evangelical Christianity" does not swing back to the imbalance prevalent in monasticism prior to the Reformation. Already Barth reveals that he sees the significance for the presence of institutional monasticism in

---

9. Barth, *Church Dogmatics* IV/2, 5.
10. Ibid., 9.
11. Ibid., 11.

"Evangelical life and thinking." However, Barth wants to distinguish the leading lights of historical monasticism from the "lesser and sometimes very small successors." This is necessary in order to separate the wheat from the chaff of monastic theology and practice, since the goal is to voice serious objections "to the ancient and modern theory and practice . . . of Eastern and Western monasticism . . . yet without invalidating in any way the underlying will and intention." The bright lights that Barth holds up for emulation and study are Macarius the Great, Basil of Caesarea, Benedict of Nursia, Francis of Assisi, Dominic, Thomas à Kempis, Ignatius of Loyola, and Theresa of Ávila, though he begins literally at the beginning, with an etymology of the word *monk*.

Noting that the English word *monk* comes from the Greek word *monos* ("alone"), Barth suggests that such a longing for being alone is not necessarily a need to flee the world, though it certainly is a kind of flight. Barth perceptively notes that there is not a necessary cultural impetus for a person's flight, so he resists the common temptation to talk in terms of how evil the third century world was that could cause such a rush of persons to the Egyptian deserts. To illustrate this point, Barth suggests that John Bunyan, the English Baptist author of the *Pilgrim's Progress* (1675), engages in a flight from the world when he leaves his family in the metaphorical City of Destruction to ascend Mount Zion. In fact, as Barth states, one does not even need to be a Christian to desire an escape from the world and, more importantly, a "flight from the world is not in any sense identical with the flight to God." Thus, Barth believes that the third century rush to the desert by "hundreds and thousands" of men and women was not culturally motivated, but simply a human response to the real or perceived transitoriness and emptiness of life, and that it grew out of an earlier practice in the apostolic age to engage in ascetic activity (not marrying, not holding possessions, and restricting one's diet) "for the edification of the [earliest Christian] congregations and for . . . sacrificial activity and concern for the destitute and sick." This communal focus, however, did not manifest itself in any particular forms of community living, believes Barth. Monks and nuns living in community was a later development and still one that should only be practiced with "the special assistance of grace."

Moving beyond the institutional aspects of monasticism, Barth progresses to the "material question," which is whether the need to withdraw from the world only has a negative connotation. That is, can one's flight from the world be seen in positive terms and not only "as an indolent and ultimately self-seeking retreat into oneself." Barth thinks that there are positive reasons for one to take flight from the world into the desert and that it could be done in protest and in opposition to the world per se, including flight from a worldly church, for the purpose of making a more effective attack against the world and the church. He bluntly states, "It might well be the law of the Spirit to which regard was had in the form of these withdrawals and the possibility of new and better Christian action which was sought and found in them." The proof of such an "attack" is in the debt that European civilization owes to the Benedictine monks and nuns and the role that some monastics had in European political life. Ultimately, for Barth, the most important question that has to be asked is whether or not all genuine Christian existence involves some sort of retreat or separation from the world for the purpose of reengaging: "Can there be either for the Church or for individuals any genuine approach to the world or men unless there is an equally genuine retreat?" Yet Barth is not naïve about the monastic life, admitting that what came to be seen as most disagreeable to many was the inordinate emphasis on excessive asceticism.

Though withdrawal was originally seen as a kind of retreat for the purpose of re-attacking, it came to be an end in itself and, worse, the result of certain fears: fear of a man and woman engaging in unlawful sexual activity, fears that one's money and possessions would keep one actively involved in the affairs of the world, and fears that the traditional vows of chastity and poverty would become meaningless if not entered into the most ascetical manner manageable. Barth writes, however, that the root of the Greek word *askesis* "simply means exercise or training for the successful attainment of a goal." If the original meaning of the word *askesis* can be recovered and asceticism can regain a proper balance, then even ascetical activity can serve the greater end of one's flight from the world, including one's liberation from excessive sin. The liberation achieved by such asceticism would "serve the redemptive and exclusively necessary freedom of man for God and his fellows, for the Church and therefore for the world." The few who can achieve such ascetic freedom are those whom we call the monks and the nuns, and these men and women keep before the church the biblical truth that the world and its lusts are passing away. Importantly, though, this is not always the case with institutionalized forms of monasticism, but that should not detract from the fact that this is true, says Barth. Barth strongly states that monasticism, as a "consistent orientation" of grace to minister to other grace-filled individuals, "cannot be suppressed."

Monasticism was the church's response to the very early problem of the "de-eschatologising and secularising of its life and message," so that when some members chose sleepiness and indolence, the church would still have her vigilant and diligent members by way of her monks and nuns. Nonetheless, this should not have resulted necessarily, writes Barth, in an institutionalization of monasticism, nor should it have manifested itself in "distinctions between the perfect and imperfect, or gradations of calling." Barth states clearly, "Monasticism was no doubt in error when it expected relief and a solution by the simple sealing off of these spheres [of sex and property]." Despite this tendency, evidenced throughout Christian history, there are still those monastics who are to be applauded and emulated. In glowing language, Barth praises "the normal monk":

> It is still patent that there always existed what we might call the normal monk whose life did not at all consist in an unceasing conflict with the different *libidines* [i.e., lusts] of the flesh, but could and can be relatively quiet and continuously and richly and fruitfully occupied with spiritual and physical labour, with all kinds of arts and serious scholarship, with the exercise of hospitality and works of charity, even with preaching and pastoral work among the people, with social work and teaching, and above all with the supremely monastic *opus Dei* [i.e., work of God], the *officium* [i.e., the daily office of prayer], the adoration of God in private and communal worship, and above and beyond all this ... with a whole range of other and very inward problems of individual and social morality.[12]

In short, Barth certainly agrees that in spirit, if not always in its institutional form, monasticism should exist. Despite its limitations, it is an expression of the Christian faith and is a genuine movement from below to above, demonstrating the reconciliation of humankind with God in Jesus Christ. The monastery is a representation of the communion of saints, which set an example to the church and world by serving both church and world. For, "what is impossible with men is possible with God, and the Spirit bloweth where he listeth, it cannot finally be disputed that a genuine fellowship of the saints could and can take place in the form of genuine commanding and genuine obeying even in the sphere of this kind of institution"—that is, monasticism.

---

12. Ibid., 15–16.

To conclude, Barth continues by affirming that monasticism "was never the den of arrogance and tyranny that the majority of Protestants imagine." Rather, there were, and are, good monasteries. Therefore, "we cannot reject out of hand the recognisable purpose of the *vita monastica*." Furthermore, the communion of the saints, the church, is surely recognized in the "distinctive triangle" of God, human and fellow humankind; and it is in the monastery that these relationships are surely nurtured by way of regular prayer and charitable service. Again, it is worth quoting Barth directly:

> The desire and aim of monasticism was to achieve in its own distinctive way a form of that discipleship of the Lord which is not only commanded generally in the Gospels but partially at least, and by way of illustration, more specifically outlined. Its desire and aim was, therefore, a concrete individual and collective sanctification, a teleological concretion of the Christian status, a practical and regulated brotherhood, and all this in the service of concrete and total love.[13]

What Barth rejects is any view of monasticism that would see it as a salvific institution, a form of assistance in one's justification. For Barth, the believer is justified by faith alone, not faith alongside monasticism, no matter how centered in the Gospel or love that monasticism may be. Monasticism issues from faith and concerns itself not with faith but with discipleship, sanctification, community, and love. Because of this, there is no reason to suppress or neglect monasticism, though the church may question the ways in which it has manifested itself historically. That being the case, that monasticism is a valuable institution and worthy of acceptance, "we can concede to the purposes and even the enterprises of monasticism."

Barth echoed this understanding of monasticism ten years later when he was asked by the abbots of the Roman Catholic Benedictine Confederation to respond to several questions about monastic life. On February 15, 1966, Barth was asked by the abbot-coadjutor, Gabriel M. Brasó, from the Benedictine abbey of Montserrat in Spain, to offer short responses to three questions: 1) what do you think of the nature of the monastic life (not the religious life generally, but specifically monastic life)?; 2) what do you believe that the church expects today from the monks?; and 3) where has, in your opinion, the *aggiornamento* of monasticism come into existence, which direction should it follow and by which basic rules is it spread?[14]

---

13. Ibid., 18.

14. *Aggiornamento* is an Italian word that means "bringing up to date." It became the

The cause of Brasó's letter was the congress of abbots of the Benedictine Confederation, who were meeting alongside the Second Vatican Council in Rome in September 1966. The council was demanding an *aggiornamento* of the monastic life but was unsure of how to proceed. Brasó, who led one of the preparation commissions of the congress of abbots, asked not only Barth, but also a number of representatives of other confessions, as well as Roman Catholic theologians, philosophers, and bishops. The fifty-six statements that resulted were published in their original languages in a volume published by the abbey of Montserrat and titled *Visioni attuali sulla vita monastica*.[15] Barth sent his reply to Brasó ten days after the inquiry, on February 25, 1966. He spoke as a "Protestant Christian and theologian." Given that the volume itself is rare and that Barth's responses have never been translated into English, it is worth discussing them fully.

Barth begins by thanking the abbots for their invitation to comment on the "monastic life and its problems today," even though he is a Protestant Christian and theologian. Moreover, he assures them that he will respond to their questions from his own theological position. This leads Barth to make seven statements. First, he says that the phrase "monastic life" must be understood as a reference to a particular person, who through a definite life-act (*Lebenstat*) has given himself or herself to a unique service; this offering of self is the result of a special gifting of the Holy Spirit. The key word for Barth here is that the monastic life is a life of *service*, implying that it is for the sake of others and not entered into egotistically or selfishly. This reflects his statements in the *Church Dogmatics* that one's withdrawal from the world is for the purpose of reentering the world in service to the church and the world. Barth was critical of what he referred to in *The Christian Life* as "principal monasticism." In this view, one attempts to be a witness to the world by staying away from it as far as possible, which results in the ability for the monk or nun to speak back into the world: the monk "wants to be as distant as he can so that in the language of the facts created by him in this distance and isolation he can stir the world to see a dimension alien to it, giving indirect visibility to the new and different thing that as a Christian he has to represent among it."[16] Barth questions

---

touchpoint and slogan of the Second Vatican Council that was seeking to reform all areas of Roman Catholic faith and practice. In non-Italian theological texts, the word remains untranslated and has become an accepted theological term.

15. Barth's contribution is found on 43–44.
16. Barth, *Christian Life*, 197.

this approach, however, wondering if one could still be a strong witness to the world without disengaging from it. Based on this thoughts in the *Church Dogmatics* and in his essay for the Benedictine abbots, it seems that Barth thought that a monk must leave the world, but only for the purpose of coming back into the world. The monk was not to remain aloof from the world permanently, but was to reengage as necessary. The solitary aspect of monasticism implied in its etymological origin (*monos* = alone) was, ironically, for the whole world.

Second, those who enter into the monastic life do so for a special *community* and this is why they are referred to as brothers and sisters, for they are in familial relationship to one another and not acting as individuals. This communal emphasis aligns well with Barth's statement in the *Church Dogmatics* that the monastic fellowship is "a fraternity in which the commonly elected abbot occupies the place of the father."[17] Monastic obedience, says Barth, involves a community and not an individual.

Third, particular monastic forms of service are based on a community's special *order*, *apostolate*, and *objective*. That is, in service to the world and the church, each monastic community expresses itself according to its own unique organization, goals, and purposes. Not all monastic communities are the same, but the work of any monastic community is defined by and defines their monastic ethos.

Fourth, the monastic life serves as an example: "The 'monastic' life of these people, their special service, their special communion with each other, their special order, approach and goal at fixing their *raison d'être*, their spirit and their right is that, depending on their place by way of *example* in the life of the wider *church*, they all represent the people of God and the Body of Christ. They are exemplary, the brothers and sisters of *all* Christians." Though worded differently, this emphasis corresponds with Barth's statement in the *Church Dogmatics* that the monks and nuns are an image of the communion of saints. They should and must be an example to the church.

Fifth, not only are monastics to be an example to the church, but they are to be an example to the world. Outside the church, the monastic life is an "active witness" to the Father, Son, and Holy Spirit, by which humanity is reconciled to God. Just as monks and nuns are "the brothers and sisters of all *Christians*," they are also "the brothers and sisters of all *people*." Again, this is consistent with Barth's comments in the *Church Dogmatics* that the

17. Barth, *Church Dogmatics* IV/2, 17.

monastic, ascetic retreat from the world is for the purpose of returning to the world. For Barth, monastics are to do this in a redemptive manner.

Sixth, a "special 'monastic' existence stands or falls" with the fact that God "in every new age and situation" re-founds new monastic expressions and assigns new persons who are "open, willing, and ready" to be obedient to God and enter into the monastic life. All this he does by his free grace. This is why Barth sees the Reformation's dismissal of monasticism as unfortunate, because the "good" monastic life is a gift of the Holy Spirit and a movement of God, not an egotistical or self-centered endeavor. Though Barth acknowledges that there were "bad" forms of monasticism, he is committed to the material form of monasticism, as stated in the *Church Dogmatics*. Furthermore, this ongoing call of individuals to the monastic life throughout church history is not contrary to or in competition with the general calling of individuals to be Christians. In *Church Dogmatics* volume three, part four, Barth speaks directly to this calling in a section on vocation. In dialogue with the German historian Karl Holl, Barth agrees that Luther's comments on 1 Corinthians 7:20 ("Each one should remain in the condition in which he was called") were intended to show that, instead of monasticism being a special vocation within the church, much less one that is superior to other vocations, the Christian's true calling is to pursue one's work within the world, not monastically apart from it. The Apostle Paul's understanding of calling had to do with one's Christian vocation and one's redemption, not one's particular calling to a specific vocation. Barth writes, "Prior to the Reformation, apart from a few variant interpretations by German Mystics in the late Middle Ages . . . call, or vocation, was taken in the basic New Testament sense of the special divine calling of man to become Christian." Though Barth affirms God's calling of specific individuals to the monastic life, this is not against God's general call upon all humankind to be reconciled to God. The problem for Barth is that the Reformation took this recovery of the Pauline sense of calling/vocation too far, so far in fact that "Protestantism successfully expelled monasticism by recalling the fact that *klēsis* [calling or vocation] is the presupposition of all Christian existence."[18]

Seventh, and lastly, despite each monastic community's special and historic apostolate, what the world and church needs and expects from her is that *primarily* she continues to speak forth and exist in accordance with the Word of God, "as witnessed in the *Holy Scriptures* of the Old and

18. Barth, *Church Domatics* III/4, 601–2.

Reforming the Monastery

New Testament." Monasticism, says Barth, has been doing this and must continue to do so, for monasticism is the same yesterday, today, and tomorrow. Monasticism's contribution to the *aggiornamento* called for by the Second Vatican Council is to be a biblically centered prophetic voice in the church and the world. As stated above, Barth, writing in his *Theology of John Calvin* in 1922, had already spoken about the prophetic voice of monasticism. There Barth says that monasticism initially "questioned and even attacked a self-assured and worldly Christianity" and it was "an uplifted finger to remind people that we cannot have the kingdom of God so cheaply." In response, room was made for the ascetical-monastic life, yet in time this prophetic voice became moot and helped to declare the triumphs of the worldly church instead of protesting against it. Barth goes so far as to say the Reformation, as a prophetic cry against a worldly church, was "an extension of the monastic line," that the Reformation's concern with true penitence "was a variation on a typically monastic question." This forced monasticism to break out of the cloister and enter into the world in order to "question the world, not as before from outside, but from inside, not in the form of the ascetic lifestyle of the few, but in that of a cross lifted up in the life of all."[19] Just as monasticism was at one time prophetic, so was the Reformation. Like Martin Luther, Barth sees the Reformation as a continuation of the monastic vocation.

From this survey of Barth's writings, it is clear to see that he was, at times, critical of some of the historical manifestations of monasticism, but considered that, as a movement of the Holy Spirit, the institution of monasticism was of benefit to the church and existed for the church and the world. Like others before him, Barth grieved the loss of monasticism in the post-Reformation Protestant church, advocating for the reestablishment of monasticism in his own time and in his own German Protestant church. This is evidenced particularly in two actions. First, in 1967 Barth read two books by Josef Böni, the former radical Roman Catholic anti-Semite who had converted to the Reformed faith. Barth had received the books from Otto Lauterburg, a Swiss pastor, but was unimpressed by the books saying that he "found neither the personality of the author congenial nor the intellectual level of his work impressive."[20] He further admits that the books annoyed him because he was recently involved in writing an article for the newspaper *National-Zeitung* opposing the Swiss Confederation's disal-

19. Barth, *Theology of John Calvin*, 50–51.
20. Barth, *Letters, 1961–1968*, 266.

lowal of the reintroduction in Switzerland of Jesuit houses and monasteries. While Böni supported retaining the clauses, Barth believed that they should be removed. Article 51 of the Federal Constitution, approved on May 29, 1874, itself states that the "order of the Jesuits, and the societies affiliated with them, shall not be received into any part of Switzerland; and all action in church and school is forbidden to its members. This prohibition may be extended also, by federal ordinance, to other religious orders, the action of which is dangerous to the state or disturbs the peace between sects." Article 52 stipulates that the "foundation of new convents or religious orders, and the reestablishment of those which have been suppressed, are forbidden." Barth's openness to seeing the reintroduction of Jesuit and other monastic houses indicates that Barth took tangible actions to support his belief that monasteries should exist, even in primarily Protestant countries.

Barth began his defense of the reintroduction of Jesuit and monastic houses in Switzerland by reminding his readers that Article 49 of the same constitution granted Swiss citizens the freedom of religion and belief. The article states that no one can be forced to participate in a religious association, therefore the presence of the Jesuits and monastic orders would not violate the constitution, because no one could be forced into these institutions, nor would they be required to support them since the article maintains that "no one shall be bound to pay taxes the proceeds of which are specifically appropriated to cover the cost of worship within a religious community to which he does not belong." Barth continues by recalling the important and radical elements of the Reformation that wrought extreme religious change in the world, including Switzerland, and how those changes were accepted. He then asks whether or not Switzerland is able to allow her citizens to engage in both ordinary and extraordinary forms of religious life, including vowed religious life. For the readers' benefit, Barth gives a brief description of monasteries and explains what, in particular, characterizes the Jesuit order. Echoing his understanding of monastic life as outlined in the *Church Dogmatics*, Barth acknowledges that there were "degenerated or feral monastic communities" historically, but suggests that this is true of the church in general and is not unique to monasticism or vowed religious life. Were the Jesuits so dangerous to the state and to the peace of nineteenth-century Switzerland that they needed to be banned? No, says Barth. Rather, such an erroneous history was a mythological evil created by those who feared the Roman Catholic Church and her influence, so much so, says Barth, that they engaged in "witch hunts." Given such a sordid history, Barth believes that the Swiss had to remedy the situation by removing the restrictions. Barth rejects the argument that if the Jesuits and monastic orders were allowed to return that they would grow rapidly and do harm to the Reformed church in Switzerland. On the contrary, Barth writes that the Reformed churches were "in their worship, their preaching, their education, their community life, their theology quiet—fixed and mobile at the same time—to their own thing." They have nothing to fear from the Jesuits and Roman Catholic monastic orders. Though it did not happen in his lifetime, Articles 51 and 52 were finally repealed in 1973. Another way in which Barth concretely demonstrated his desire to see monastic institutes return to the Protestant church was by way of his support for religious communities and for those in support of the religious life. Perhaps the greatest example of this would be Barth's partner in the Confessing Church, the Lutheran theologian Dietrich Bonhoeffer.

DIETRICH BONHOEFFER

Dietrich Bonhoeffer was born on February 4, 1906. After studies at the University of Tübingen, he earned his PhD at the age of twenty-one from the Alexander von Humboldt University in Berlin. Bonhoeffer spent most of his life serving as a pastor and professor in Spain, London, and Germany. With the rise of Nazism in the late 1920s and early 1930s, Bonhoeffer took an active role in the Confessing Church—the church that emerged as an alternative to the Aryanization of the German Evangelical Church. In Helmuth Gollwitzer's words, "The Confessing Church is the confessing remnant of the German Evangelical Church."[21] In 1937, he became the director of the underground Confessing Church seminary at Finkenwalde. Bonhoeffer was arrested in 1944, primarily for his work in helping German Jews escape to Switzerland and for his work with the Abwehr, a German military intelligence organization that was also the center of resistance to Adolph Hitler. Bonhoeffer was condemned to die on April 8, 1945 and was hanged on April 9, 1945 at the Flossenbürg concentration camp.

Barth and Bonhoeffer met for the first time in July 1931 and continued to meet periodically throughout the remainder of Bonhoeffer's life. As a student, Bonhoeffer had read Barth's works extensively, being sympathetic yet critical of Barth's theology. In an exchange of letters from 1936, we see Barth and Bonhoeffer discussing the religious life. At this time,

21. Quoted in Bonhoeffer, *Way to Freedom*, 104.

Karl Barth and Dietrich Bonhoeffer

Bonhoeffer was serving as director of the Confessing Church's seminary at Finkenwalde and he is cognizant of the fact that the seminarians need to focus on learning how to pray and read the Bible, though some think that the focus of the seminarians should be on learning to preach and catechize. In response, Bonhoeffer writes, "That seems to me either a complete misunderstanding of what young theologians are like today or a culpable ignorance of how preaching and catechism come to life. The questions that are seriously put to us today by young theologians are: How do I learn to pray? How do I learn to read the Bible? If we cannot help them there we cannot help them at all."[22] For Bonhoeffer, "both theological work and real pastoral fellowship can only grow in a life which is governed by gathering round the Word morning and evening and by fixed times of prayer." Not only does Bonhoeffer see great value in teaching seminarians how to pray and read the Bible, but he also, in the same letter, places a great value on living in community together. In reply, Barth expressed concern about what he calls the "distinction in principle between theological work and devotional edification which is evident . . . from your letter." Further, Barth is concerned about the "almost indefinable odour of a monastic eros and pathos" that he senses has taken over at the seminary. It would seem that Barth views monasticism negatively in this letter, but we have seen above how he was more positive about the institution of monasticism in the early 1930s. Perhaps, then, Barth's concern here has more to do with the mode of education at the seminary than with monasticism *qua* monasticism. What is clear, however, is that Bonhoeffer is engaging in some form of community living and praying that appears monastic. Yet, what were Bonhoeffer's views of monasticism at this time? To answer this question, we will turn to his *Cost of Discipleship* and *Life Together*.

The Cost of Discipleship was published in 1937, so Bonhoeffer was working on the book when he wrote the abovementioned letter to Barth. In fact, he says that he is working on the book in the letter to Barth. In this work, Bonhoeffer is concerned with "the obedient deeds of discipleship in response to God's word in Jesus Christ."[23] His emphasis throughout is on "costly grace" as opposed to "cheap grace." Bonhoeffer writes that

> Cheap grace is preaching forgiveness without repentance; it is baptism without the discipline of community; it is the Lord's Supper without confession of sin; it is absolution without personal

---

22. This quotation and the following come from Bonhoeffer, *Way to Freedom*, 117–21.
23. Bonhoeffer, *Discipleship*, 6. Hereafter cited parenthetically by page number.

Reforming the Monastery

> confession. Cheap grace is grace without discipleship, grace without the cross, grace without the living, incarnate Jesus Christ. (44)

Costly grace, on the other hand, "is costly, because it calls to discipleship; it is grace, because it calls us to follow *Jesus Christ*" (45). For Bonhoeffer, costly grace guided the life of Jesus' first disciples and is evidenced in such moments as when the apostle Peter leaves his fishing business because Jesus has called him (Mark 1:16–18). Against this backdrop, on several occasions in the work Bonhoeffer takes up a discussion of monasticism.

According to Bonhoeffer, the loss of costly grace is the result of the expansion of the Christian church and the "increasing secularization of the church" (46). Thus, as the world became Christian, or at least nominally so, grace became the common property of all people. This led to the cheapening of grace. Yet, there was one institution that maintained a concept of costly grace: monasticism. As Bonhoeffer writes, "It was decisive that monasticism did not separate from the church and that the church had the good sense to tolerate monasticism. Here, on the boundary of the church, was the place where the awareness that grace is costly and that grace includes discipleship was preserved" (46). Monastic life stood against the secularization of Christianity and, by extension, the cheapening of grace. However, Bonhoeffer goes on to say that because the church allowed the institution of monasticism, it relativized it, because monasticism became the place where individuals exercised extraordinary achievements that were not open to most Christians. Thus, the

> fateful limiting of the validity of Jesus' commandments to a certain group of especially qualified people led to differentiating between highest achievement and lowest performance in Christian obedience. This made it possible, when the secularization of the church was attacked any further, to point to the possibility of the monastic way within the church, alongside which another possibility, that of an easier way, was also justified. (47)

Seen in this light, the mistake of monasticism was that it created a way for a select few to become extraordinary, thus claiming a special kind of merit for itself.

Ironically, it seems for Bonhoeffer, the reawakening of the gospel and costly grace at the Reformation came about by a monk—Martin Luther. Bonhoeffer believes that Luther invested his whole life in his monastic calling, but that he failed to live up to the standards set before him. This allowed Luther to see that "discipleship is not the meritorious achievements of individuals, but a divine commandment to all Christians" (47). In his failure as a monk, Luther was able to be seized by grace again, but this time is was clear that he needed to move beyond himself and his ascetic achievements and move forward only through God's enabling grace: "Luther had to leave the monastery and reenter the world, not because the world itself was good and holy, but because even the monastery was nothing else but world" (48). Due to this realization, it occurred to Luther that what had once been practiced only in the cloister now had to be what was necessary for all Christians. The costly grace of the monastery had now exploded back into the world. In short, for Bonhoeffer, elitist monasticism was its own greatest enemy, since it created two classes of Christian citizens: those living according to costly grace (monastics) and those living according to cheap grace (non-monastics).

Bonhoeffer, however, is not saying that the very institution of monasticism should be abolished. Rather, Bonhoeffer believes that Luther's greatest insight is that the demands of the monastery are for all people. Luther recovered that which had been lost because of a misdirected monasticism. Luther "did not repudiate the very lofty standards set by monastic life, but that obedience to the command of Jesus was understood as an achievement of individuals," writes Bonhoeffer. Furthermore, "Luther did not attack the 'unworldliness' of monastic life, but the fact that within the confines of the monastery this estrangement from the world had been turned into a new spiritual conformity to this world" (245). For Luther, according to Bonhoeffer, monasticism as an institution needed to be reformed, since it came to be an instrument of the secularization of Christianity and therefore an instrument of cheap grace. Yet, Bonhoeffer himself held the institution of monasticism in high enough esteem to write elsewhere that the "restoration of the church will surely come from a sort of new monasticism which has in common with the old only the uncompromising attitude of a life lived according to the Sermon on the Mount in the following of Christ. I believe it is now time to call people to this."[24]

Bonhoeffer's greatest support for the monastic life came in his *Life Together*. In the summer of 1934, when he was living and pastoring in London, Bonhoeffer was asked if he would return to Germany and be involved in the founding of preacher's seminaries for the Confessing Church. The impetus for founding such seminaries grew out of the fact that the state church, under Nazi influence, had closed the preacher's seminaries in Prussia and

---

24. Bonhoeffer, *Testament to Freedom*, 424.

Reforming the Monastery

would only let ordinands take exams if they could document their pure Aryan heritage. Bonhoeffer was torn about this invitation, since he himself was making plans to travel to India to learn from Mahatma Ghandi about community and passive resistance. In a letter to Erwin Sutz, a Swiss pastor and theologian who had studied with Karl Barth, dated September 11, 1934, Bonhoeffer talks about his struggle regarding his decision to either go to India, remain in London, or return to Germany to start a preacher's seminary. In this letter, he confesses his lack of faith in universities to provide an adequate education for future pastors. Instead, "The entire training of young seminarians belongs today in church-monastic schools in which the pure doctrine, the Sermon on the Mount, and worship can be taken seriously."[25]

Later in this same letter, Bonhoeffer expresses his desire to study how such a "monastic" training of pastors occurred in other traditions. This desire led Bonhoeffer to write to George Bell, Anglican bishop of Chichester, asking him to write letters to superiors of Anglican monastic communities and seminaries requesting hospitality for Bonhoeffer. According to Bishop Bell, Bonhoeffer was "very anxious to have some acquaintance with our methods in England, both with regard to training for the ministry and with regard to community life."[26] Bishop Bell wrote to three religious communities (the Community of the Resurrection, the Society of the Sacred Mission, and the Society of St. John the Evangelist) and to two seminaries (St. Augustine's College, Canterbury and Wycliffe Hall, Oxford). After deciding not to go to India, Bonhoeffer visited most of these communities in March 1935.

In the end, Bonhoeffer agreed to return to Germany and oversee one of the preacher's seminaries. On March 10, 1935, he preached his final sermon to his London congregations and was back in Germany around Easter. Bonhoeffer and his first students left Berlin on April 26, 1935 on their way to the abandoned facilities of the Rhineland Bible School in Zingst. However, in June of the same year, they were forced to move, choosing to settle in a former school in the village of Finkenwalde. *Life Together*, published in 1939, is Bonhoeffer's distillation of the spiritual practices of this group of students as he strove to lead them in a *vita communis*, a life of communion. Before looking at *Life Together* directly, however, it might help to lay

---

25. Bonhoeffer, *Life Together*, 12.
26. Bethge, *Dietrich Bonhoeffer*, 335.

out the way of life and difficulties of attempting to establish community at Finkenwalde.

The daily routine of life at the seminary began and ended with two services, conducted at the dinner table.[27] The services began with a series of readings: a psalm, followed by a hymn, an Old Testament lesson, and a New Testament lesson. A time of extemporaneous prayer followed the readings and the praying of the Lord's Prayer. On Saturdays, Bonhoeffer included a sermon and allowed no work to be done on Sundays. Similar to monastic practice, Bonhoeffer introduced the practice of reading aloud during meals, despite the students' complaints that this was too monkish. The students spent their days studying homiletics, church ministry, the Lutheran confessional documents, and hearing Bonhoeffer's lectures on the Sermon on the Mount that would become *The Cost of Discipleship*.

Not only was Bonhoeffer able to write while at Finkenwalde, he was also able to initiate a community within the preacher's seminary that would come to be called the "House of the Brethren." The nature of this community is summed up well by Bethge: "Bonhoeffer believed that the circumstances of the day and his own theological principles now demanded the creation for Protestants of something which, for centuries, they had known to exist only under Roman Catholic imprimatur."[28] Bethge, of course, is referring to the institution of monasticism, saying that Bonhoeffer's "House of the Brethren" was intended to be a Protestant monastery, which is exactly what he said needed to happen when he wrote to his brother on January 14, 1935 (cited above). The House would exist for four purposes. First, to make the members better preachers since, Bonhoeffer believed, communal living assisted in giving greater objectivity to one's sermons. The purpose of the House was proclamation, not contemplation. Second, the house existed to further the discipleship of its members, who could no longer only live out their Christian life abstractly. Third, by renouncing their "traditional privileges," ministers of the House would always be available for service to others. Fourth, the community could become a spiritual refuge for pastors who needed, on occasion, to make a retreat to regain strength. Bethge, who lived in the community, writes,

> The *vita communis* envisaged in the proposal was to take the form of a daily order of prayer, brotherly exhortation, free personal confession, common theological work and a very simple communal

27. Ibid., 349ff.
28. Ibid., 379.

> life. The brethren would pledge themselves to answer every emergency call from the Church and, should they wish to leave the community, they would be free to do so. Admission would be by common consent of the community.[29]

In the end, however, the Gestapo closed Finkenwalde in the fall of 1937, so both the seminary and the House of Brethren lasted fewer than three years.

It was the closure of the seminary and the House that led Bonhoeffer to write *Life Together*. The work is divided into five chapters: "Community," "The Day with Others," "The Day Alone," "Ministry and Confession," and "Communion." From this one can already discern the nature of the community that Bonhoeffer hoped to create—a life centered on love of God and neighbor, extending out from the sacraments of confession and communion. Regarding community, Bonhoeffer did not envision that his life together with others would be some sort of a cloistered life, much less one dedicated to contemplation. Rather, Christians are called not only to live among other Christians, but also "in the thick of foes."[30] It is natural, writes Bonhoeffer, for a Christian to yearn for the physical presence of other Christians. In fact, the very essence of Christianity is community in and through Jesus Christ (21). For Bonhoeffer, this means that one Christian brings the Word of God, Jesus Christ, to another Christian and vice versa. Thereby, "they meet one another as bringers of the message of salvation" (23).

Furthermore, Bonhoeffer insists that Christian community is not an ideal but is, in fact, a divine reality, and that this community is a spiritual community and not only "a psychic reality" (26). Christian community is not something that Christians strive to create, but is a reality created by God in which Christians participate. Thus, community is God's gift to his church. To create a real community of persons living together is to create an image of the community that already exists in Christ, and this community is a spiritual, pneumatic community. A successful Christian life together must recognize the difference between mere human community and divine spiritual community. In Bonhoeffer's words,

> life together under the Word will remain sound and healthy only where it does not form itself into a movement, an order, a society, a *collegium pietatis* [college of piety], but rather where it understands itself as being a part of the one, holy, catholic, Christian

---

29. Ibid., 385.
30. Bonhoeffer, *Life Together*, 17. Hereafter cited parenthetically by page number.

Church, where it shares actively and passively in the sufferings and struggles and promise of the whole Church. (37)

Bonhoeffer's chapter "The Day with Others" begins to explain how a Christian community is to be a divine, spiritual community and not merely a human, psychic association.

In community, the day begins with common praise of God, common hearing of the Word, and common prayer. In Bonhoeffer's estimation, every common devotion should include Scripture reading, church hymns, and prayer. For Bonhoeffer, the Protestant church needs to recover the practice of praying the Psalter, for it is in "the Psalter we learn to pray on the basis of Christ's prayer. The Psalter is the great school of prayer" (47). After reading the selected psalms, concluded with a hymn, the community is to read the Scriptures, including "longer" readings from the Old and New Testaments. In Bonhoeffer's estimation, a community should be able to read an entire chapter from the Old Testament and at least half a chapter from the New Testament every morning and evening. Bonhoeffer also stipulated that in the community, the Bible should be read in a continuous manner, the so-called *lectio continua*, as opposed to reading selections of various books prescribed by a lectionary. His reason for this is that the Bible is a "living whole" and must be read as a unity. Furthermore, "Consecutive reading of Biblical books forces everyone who wants to hear to put himself, or to allow himself to be found, where God has acted once and for all for the salvation of men. We become part of what once took place for our salvation" (53). Finally, states Bonhoeffer, the readings should be done by all in turns.

In addition to reciting the Psalter and reading the Bible, those living in community will also sing together. Bonhoeffer prescribes singing after both the recitation of the psalms and after the biblical readings. After the second hymn, the community gives itself to common prayers. Bonhoeffer sums up the nature of common prayer as follows:

> We have heard God's Word, and we have been permitted to join in the hymn of the Church; but now we are to pray as a fellowship, and this prayer must really be *our* word, *our* prayer for this day, for our work, for our fellowship, for the particular needs and sins that oppress us in common, for the persons who are committed to our care. (62; Bonhoeffer's italics)

Bonhoeffer believes that it is best for one person, the "head of the family," to always offer these "free" prayers. Other community members join in the common prayer by praying for the leader as he prays. As the leader makes intercession for the community, the community makes intercession for the leader. These free prayers are prayers for the community and "not that of the individual who is praying" (63). After the prayers, the final act of morning community worship is the sharing together in communion for "the daily table fellowship binds the Christians to their Lord and one another" (67).

After concluding the morning office, the remainder of the day up until evening is given to work. Here one is reminded of the Benedictine motto of *Ora et labora*—pray and work. In Bonhoeffer's estimation, prayer should not be hindered by the community's work, but neither should work be hindered by prayer. The work of the community, in this case education and pastoral ministry, "plunges men into the world of things" (70). This work is interrupted at the noon hour for a common meal and "a brief devotion of song and prayer" (73). Finally, in the evening, the community gathers together for another meal and for an evening devotion. Regarding this evening devotion Bonhoeffer writes,

> This is the appropriate place for common intercession. After the day's work we pray God for the blessing, peace, and safety of all Christendom; for our congregation; for the pastor in his ministry; for the poor, the wretched, and lonely; for the sick and dying; for our neighbors, for our own folks at home, and for our fellowship. (73)

It is also at this evening office that the community is to engage in intentional repentance, asking God to forgive the members for each wrong committed against God and others. This was done, writes Bonhoeffer, because it is "an ancient monastic custom" for an abbot to ask forgiveness from his monks and for the monks to ask forgiveness from their abbot. It would seem here especially that Bonhoeffer is making a connection between the institution of monasticism and his idea of community, showing continuity between the two.

In the chapter titled "The Day Alone," Bonhoeffer gives attention to several areas of living in community that are not structural, but spiritual. He first discusses solitude and silence. According to Bonhoeffer, he who cannot be alone should not enter into community. It is in being able to live alone that one is fully prepared to live in community. One who can stand alone before God can certainly stand before God as a member of a community, where he is no longer alone. Paradoxically, "only as we are within the fellowship can we be alone, and only he that is alone can live in the fellowship. Only in fellowship do we learn to be rightly alone and only in

Karl Barth and Dietrich Bonhoeffer

aloneness do we learn to live rightly in the fellowship" (77). From this place of aloneness (or solitude), emerges silence, which is the mark of solitude. Solitude is unable to exist without silence, states Bonhoeffer. Out of this silence and solitude emerges three other spiritual practices: meditation, prayer, and intercession.

In meditation, the Christian finds herself "alone with the Word" (81). In the morning and evening devotions, the community reads long passages of the Scriptures; in meditation a short text is chosen that can be meditated upon over the course of a week. For Bonhoeffer, in "meditation we ponder the chosen text on the strength of the promise that it has something utterly personal to say to us for this day and for our Christian life, that it is not only God's Word for the Church, but also God's Word for us individually" (82). Like *lectio divina*, Bonhoeffer says that one sentence or even one word may become the basis for meditation and it is not necessary for the one engaged in meditation to express her thoughts in words, but unspoken thought and prayer are as beneficial. Bonhoeffer believes that meditation leads one to prayer, for prayer is "nothing else but the readiness and willingness to receive and appropriate the Word" (84). What cannot be prayed during corporate prayer should be prayed in personal prayer. Finally, silence and solitude lends itself to intercessory prayer. Bonhoeffer recognizes that there will be more prayer needs in the community than can be prayed during the morning office. Therefore, during one's time of solitude and silence, additional prayers should be made on behalf of others in the community and outside the community also. Bonhoeffer concludes that "since meditation on the Scriptures, prayer, and intercession are a service we owe and because the grace of God is found in this service, we should train ourselves to set apart a regular hour of it" (87).

The reception of *Life Together* was mixed. Some greatly appreciated the work. Others, however, could see in it only an attempt by Bonhoeffer to reestablish monasticism in the Protestant church. In this evaluation they were correct. It is clear in the structure of the community that Bonhoeffer was thinking of the monastic daily rhythms. Already in 1934, Eberhard Arnold, founder of the German *bruderhof*, had referred to Bonhoeffer's "monastic ideas."[31] In many ways, Bonhoeffer's *Life Together* is a monastic rule similar to the rule of Benedict of Nursia. Benedict's rule also places an emphasis on the daily offices (including the reading the Psalms), regular confession and communion, silence, solitude, meditation, study, and work.

---

31. Bonhoeffer, *London, 1933–1935*, 166.

Reforming the Monastery

Bonhoeffer's *Life Together*	*Rule of Benedict*
Reading the Psalms	Chapters 8–19
Hymn(s)	Chapter 9.4; 11.8, 10; 12.4; 13.11; 17.3–5; 18.8
Scripture reading (Old and New Testaments)	Chapter 9.8; 10.2; 11.6–9; 12.4; 13.9–11; 73.3
Common/Free prayer	Chapter 20
Work	Chapter 48
Mid-day devotion	Chapter 16
Evening devotion	Chapter 16; 17.7–10; 42
Solitude/Silence	Chapter 6; 7.56–58; 38.5; 42.1; 52.2
Meditation	Chapter 8.3; 48.23; 58.5
Personal prayer	Chapter 52

In short, Dietrich Bonhoeffer had a vision for the implementation of institutionalized monasticism in the Confessing Church of Germany. Though the Nazis abruptly ended the Finkenwalde "experiment," as well as Bonhoeffer's life, it is possible to imagine that this attempt at monastic community living may have flourished had not World War II occurred. Such a reintroduction of monasticism into the Protestant German church in the twentieth century would have been consistent with its continuation after the Reformation in the sixteenth century.

Post-Reformation German Monasticism

As seen in the previous chapter on Martin Luther, although monasticism was viewed with great suspicion and even held in disdain by some, it was not completely rejected, nor did it cease to exist in post-Reformation Germany. From Reformation-era documents, such as the Augsburg Confession and the Apology of the Augsburg Confession, it can be seen that monasteries were viewed as institutions of education; therefore, the German reformers argued, monasteries should continue to exist in order to provide education for school-aged children. None of the Reformers suggested that monasteries should continue exactly as they had before the Reformation, but they did believe that they could continue to serve the church as schools.

It was not the first generation of Protestant reformers but the second that gave shape to this vision of the monasteries as schools. The directives for these institutions survive in so-called cloister orders, church orders, and school orders. In general, the orders make three suggestions regarding the monasteries: 1) the monasteries should be closed and their property and possessions should be given to the state; 2) the inhabitants should be cared for either while remaining in the monastery or in a common location chosen for those who wish to remain even after being given the opportunity to leave; and 3) the monastic life should be reformed along the theological lines of the Reformation and become an educational institution.[32] Though many monasteries ceased to exist under the first two options, some continued as monasteries. For those that continued, certain common features emerge in the cloister ordinances.

First, reformation of worship centered around holy communion, preaching, and the daily prayer offices. Holy communion was no longer allowed when only one person (i.e., the priest) was present and the canon of the communion service (i.e., that portion of the service occurring between the proper preface and the "Our Father," including the words of institution) was revised to be in conformity with Reformation theology, especially the doctrine of justification by faith. Preaching was required several days a week, whereas it was infrequent in late medieval practice. The daily offices were simplified and were prayed in both German and Latin.

Second, the taking of monastic vows (such as celibacy, poverty, and stability) was no longer allowed. Monks and nuns were allowed to leave the cloister to marry if they desired. However, obedience to the monastery's leadership was still expected, but was now promised, not vowed. Instead of the so-called evangelical counsels, promises to maintain peace and to live together in love were substituted.

Third, ceremonies and practices unique to monastic life were discarded. The monastic habit was discarded, as was the daily chapter meeting where members of the community could air their faults and grievances. Ceremonies of dedication for new members were theoretically halted, though they continued in some communities. For example, in five cloisters near Hannover, the "directress" (German: *Oberin*) gave a veil to each new member at a service performed in the church, and at Kloster Neuwerk in Goslar a head covering was placed on the new members in a so-called "cloister wedding."

Fourth, the official theological position of the monasteries had to be in agreement with the theological principles set down by Luther, Philipp

---

32. Weiser, "Communal Ministries in Lutheranism," 303. Hereafter cited parenthetically by page number.

Melanchthon, and other reformers. Official theological statements were Luther's catechism, the Augsburg Confession, or the Apology of the Augsburg Confession.

Fifth, all the ordinances state that the reason for a continued existence of the monasteries is to offer educational opportunities for children. It is stated repeatedly that the monasteries were originally "learning houses" (German: *Lehrhäuser*) and "training houses" (German: *Zuchthäuser*), therefore they should return to their original purpose. Of the three possible solutions for handling the monasteries outlined above, this is the option that was most often chosen. This is likely due to the fact that no theological rationale for the continued existence of monasteries in the Lutheran church emerged. As Weiser comments, "There is no theological justification given for the continuance of life in the cloister. In its place, in effect, the practical justification in terms of the new task [of education] is substituted for theological inquiry into the legitimacy of this way of life." Weiser also concludes that the ordinances do not hint at any sense of conflict between a reformed monastic life and Lutheran theology. Instead, "they seem to see in them a good tool for setting this doctrine firmly in the lives of the people" (304–5). This educational task expected that each member of the community take oversight of one pupil—teaching him/her writing, reading, the doctrine and worship of the church, and, in the case of young girls, work appropriate to women, such as sewing ecclesiastical garments.

The later history of many of these monasteries is one of decline. For example, many of the women's communities, especially after the Thirty Years' War, forsook the apostolates of prayer and education and became foundations for women (German: *Damenstifte*), with the only residue of community life being common attendance of worship on Sunday. The women ceased eating together and converted their cells and dormitories into individual apartments with multiple rooms. By the eighteenth century, the women were no longer wearing any distinctive dress, but wore typical eighteenth-century women's clothing. Further, as Weiser writes,

> As the royalty gained power to designate the inhabitants of the cloister . . . they used the old cloisters as homes for their unmarried aunts and sisters and nieces. And finally, by the time the nineteenth century arrived, the pattern developed so far that in a number of situations actual residence in the cloister was not even required of those so designated. (307)

In the end, the institution of monasticism would not survive in Protestant Germany.

Modern Monastic Renewal in Germany

A kind of monasticism, however, was revived in the nineteenth century German church under the leadership of Theodor Fliedner and William Loehe. In 1836, Fliedner, a member of the United Church of Prussia, opened a hospital and a deaconess training center, having recognized the need for this institution and after exposure to Moravian deaconesses. Fliedner believed that a married woman could not be an effective deaconess, since marriage was already too demanding of their time. He therefore opened a motherhouse so that single women could live together in community, appointed himself as the *paterfamilias* over the community, and had the women adopt the standard dress of a married woman so that the deaconess would be accepted socially, like married women. In Weiser's estimation, these deaconesses were equivalent to a Roman Catholic religious order: Fliedner "succeeded in creating a Protestant religious community, modeled in many ways upon the Roman Catholic Sisters of Charity" (309). The life of the deaconesses involved both prayer and work. A deaconess' day would begin and end with corporate worship with medical, domestic, or educational work at other times.

It was the Lutheran Wilhelm Loehe who built upon the work of Fliedner, making the deaconess movement part of the Lutheran church in Germany. According to Weiser, Loehe's strong Protestantism at first made him reluctant to think of the deaconesses as a sisterhood and simply thought of them as associations of professionals. In time, however, he accepted the concept of a Protestant sisterhood: "Brotherhoods and sisterhoods are not a sign of a dead church, but rather of the still existing good will. Thus, the present diaconate, at a time of corruption in the folk churches, is the support and pillar of spiritual life" (311). Loehe championed celibacy for the deaconesses, referring to them as the "unmarried bride[s] of my parish." Loehe believed that the Lutheran church held the married life in high esteem while holding celibacy in contempt and he saw the diaconate as an institution correcting this imbalance. He also adopted the other two historical evangelical counsels of poverty and obedience, emphasizing that the deaconesses needed to "not consider earthly goods as a personal

Reforming the Monastery

possession" and to see "every restraint of self-will . . . [as] an invitation to genuine freedom." In vivid language, Loehe describes the deaconesses:

> The black dress . . . signifies renunciation of the world. A deaconess is done with the gaily-colored pomp of the world. The white apron our deaconesses have taken from the greatest of all deacons, our Lord Jesus, since he washed his disciples' feet. They have selected this humble garb for their festival and Communion vestment. In daily life, learning and working they wear the same apron in blue, as a sign of perseverance and faithfulness. On their heads, the deaconesses and students wear a white veil for going to the offices and on festival occasions. They wear it not simply because it warms and protects and is cheaper and more beautiful than a hat or cap but also because this veil on her head reminds her that she has given herself to the eternal bridegroom, Christ, so long as it pleases him. And he leads her nowhere else but to serve his poor and helpless ones. (312)

For Loehe, the deaconess was one with Christ through her servanthood and through her "marriage" to Christ, the heavenly bridegroom. This vision of institutional religious life harkens back to the Roman Catholic religious orders of the pre- and post-Reformation era. Yet, the deaconesses are not the only religious orders in the modern Lutheran church.

In 1942, a young group of women resolved to engage in evangelistic outreach to other young women, despite being outlawed by the Nazis. On Easter night, they promised "fidelity to my Lord, Jesus Christ. His Gospel will be my rule of life." In time, members began to live in community under the direction of the Benedictine monk Theophil Lamm of Münsterschwarzach Abbey in Würzburg. By 1950, this group of women was living together in a community and was received as a monastery in 1958 by the council and bishop of the Lutheran church in Bavaria, under the name of Communität Casteller Ring. This community follows the Rule of Benedict and takes vows of chastity, common ownership of all property and obedience. The sisters have four fixed prayer times each day—morning, midday, evening, and night—and they worship as a community three times each week (Sunday, Tuesday, and Friday), celebrating the Eucharist together at each of these services. Their work consists of educational endeavors (including a conference center), spiritual direction and, since 1996, operating and maintaining Martin Luther's former Augustinian priory in Erfurt, Germany.

Between 1936 and 1944, two women, Klara Schlink and Erica Madauss, started several Bible study groups near Darmstadt for young women that had begun as residential Bible study courses for future clergy wives. By 1944, there were about 150 young women involved in the studies. On the night of September 11–12, 1944, there was an air raid on Darmstadt by Allied forces that, in twenty minutes, nearly wiped out all of Darmstadt, killing thirty thousand people. Many of the young women in the Bible studies saw this as God's judgment and sign that he was calling them to repentance and prayer for their own sins and the sins of the German nation. The Ecumenical Community of the Sisters of Mary was officially founded on March 30, 1947, after many of the sisters came to realize their desire to live in community under the guidance of Methodist pastor Paul Reidinger. The community adopted the name "Sisters of Mary" in allusion to the way of faith and obedience that Mary, the mother of Jesus, showed to the will of God. Klara Schlink changed her name to Mother Basilea, and Erica Madauss came to be known as Mother Martyria; they led the community until their deaths in 2001 and 1999, respectively. The community gathers daily for prayer (historically gathering for the full sevenfold monastic office) and is involved in various forms of ecumenical work and reconciliation ministries. They have spread across the world with communities in the United States, Canada, Australia, Brazil, Japan, and elsewhere.

In 1967, the Priory of Saint Wigbert was founded as a confraternity of Lutheran craftsmen. They relocated to Wernigshausen (near Erfurt) in 1973 and began to tear down decrepit churches and repair others. Choosing to live according to the Rule of Benedict, it was not until 1987 that bishop Werner Leich, of the Evangelical Lutheran Church in Thuringia, approved their monastic way of life. The community gathers together to pray four times each day (morning, midday, evening, and night) and once each week for the Eucharist (on Thursday). The community is now made up of fewer than ten members, two of whom are Roman Catholic Christians. They are actively engaged in ecumenical work, along with serving several parish churches in the area.

Though many more monasteries could be discussed, this small sampling suffices to demonstrate that the monastic theology of Karl Barth and Dietrich Bonhoeffer has, in fact, manifested itself in monastic institutions in Germany and even in the larger Lutheran church.[33] Though Barth and Bonhoeffer both had nuanced and articulate views of monasticism as an institution, it was left to later Lutheran leaders to bring new communities

---

33. See Rinderknecht, "Discovering a Common Life," and the list of Protestant religious orders at http://www.orden-online.de/linkverzeichnis/index.php?rubrik_id=15.

Reforming the Monastery

to light. The number of communities and the rapidity with which they are emerging is a testament to the reforming of the monastery in historically Protestant Lutheranism.

FOUR

Donald Bloesch and the Evangelical Tradition

"The perennial question in systematic theology is the role of the Christian life in our salvation." So begins the inaugural address of Donald Bloesch as an Associate Professor of Theology at the Theological Seminary of the University of Dubuque, Iowa, on February 7, 1962, setting the stage in some measure for a lifelong interest not only in the Christian life in general, but also in the religious life in particular. The inaugural address continues by arguing that "the Christian life does not purchase salvation, but it is the arena in which our salvation is carried forward to victory." For Bloesch, the order of salvation is a paradox in which one affirms "that we in ourselves contribute nothing to our salvation; yet in Christ we contribute everything." He concludes, against traditional Reformed theology, that the salvation of humankind is completely dependent upon God while also completely dependent upon each person: "We can obey only through the power of the cross; the cross becomes efficacious only as we obey. . . . Both parts of this proposition must be affirmed if we are to do justice to the dynamic and paradoxical nature of Christian salvation." Given the significance of such theological conclusions at the beginning of his teaching and publishing career, it is not unexpected that Bloesch would continue throughout the years to return to the topic of the Christian life. In fact, not only does he return to the topic of the Christian life frequently and systematically, but also he repeatedly discusses one aspect of the Christian life in particular—monasticism. This is logical, given Bloesch's understanding that one's doctrinal theology must be held in balance with one's theology of the spiritual life. It is likely that this integral connection between theology and the spiritual life is the result of Bloesch's own personal and theological formation.

Reforming the Monastery

Donald G. Bloesch was born in Bremen, Indiana, on May 3, 1928, to a family of Swiss descendants sent as Christian missionaries to the United States to serve German-speaking immigrants. His father was a pastor in the German Evangelical Church and a member of the Evangelical Synod of North America. In 1934, the Evangelical Synod merged with the Reformed Church in the United States to form the Evangelical and Reformed Church. This denomination later joined the Congregational Christian Churches, which created the United Church of Christ. In 1946, Bloesch began his undergraduate studies at Elmhurst College in Illinois, majoring in philosophy. Upon graduation from Elmhurst, Bloesch entered Chicago Theological Seminary (CTS) to pursue the call to Christian ministry that came to him during his high school years and to pursue a concentration in the sociology of religion. At CTS, Bloesch encountered what he characterized as an extreme liberal theology that was prevalent in the seminary at that time. Bloesch also encountered neoorthodoxy—a theological perspective grounded in historical Reformed theology while taking seriously contemporary cultural and theological developments—and read works by Søren Kierkegaard, Emil Brunner, Karl Barth, Paul Tillich, Rudolph Bultmann, and Reinhold Niebuhr. Also, while in Chicago, Bloesch participated in the InterVarsity Christian Fellowship chapter, sharing, he says, in that group a bond that he did not have with other students at CTS. This, aided by the influence of his maternal grandmother, helped to preserve Bloesch from surrendering completely to the liberal theology surrounding him.

After graduating from CTS in 1953 with a thesis titled "Emil Brunner's Approach to Non-Christian Religions," Bloesch was ordained on June 23, 1954, at Nazareth Evangelical and Reformed Church in Chicago, Illinois, while already serving as a licensed minister at St. Paul's United Church of Christ in Richton Park, Illinois. He continued in this pastorate from 1953 to 1956 while a doctoral student at the University of Chicago Divinity School. At the University of Chicago, Bloesch studied under the philosopher of religion and metaphysician Charles Hartshorne, church historian Wilhelm Pauck, historical theologian Jaroslav Pelikan, and process theologian Daniel Day Williams. When nearing completion of his doctoral dissertation, Bloesch learned that his thesis advisor, Williams, was leaving the university. Williams' replacement, the religious philosopher Bernard Meland, was not interested in Bloesch's topic. This forced Bloesch to write a new dissertation, titled "Reinhold Niebuhr's Re-Evaluation of the Apologetic Task," which he successfully defended in 1956.

Donald Bloesch and the Evangelical Tradition

After completing his PhD, Bloesch spent the following year doing postdoctoral work at Oxford University through a scholarship from the World Council of Churches. While at Oxford, Bloesch exposed himself to the religious life of the Anglo-Catholic monasteries, which, he later said, left a lasting impression on him. Fascinated by these British monastics, Bloesch visited (primarily Protestant) religious houses in Switzerland, France, Italy, and Germany, resulting in his first book, *Centers of Christian Renewal* (1964). Because of his visits to these European religious communities and his own academic work in the area, Bloesch has remained fascinated with expressions of religious community life. He has always viewed these communities as centers for genuine spiritual renewal in the Christian church and always maintained that these institutions are necessary in the Protestant church.

On the other hand, Bloesch has reported that he reacted somewhat negatively to the ascetic rigorism found in some of the forms of monasticism that he encountered. As well, in those Anglo-Catholic monasteries of Oxford, Bloesch felt "turned off" because of what he perceived to be a tendency towards works-righteousness. In fact, over the course of his scholarly career, Bloesch has provided a number of reasons why one could reject the institution of monasticism. For example, in his *Struggle of Prayer*, he writes,

> The eremitic and monastic ways are constantly threatened by a false kind of mysticism in which one's attention is turned away from the anguish of the world to the vision of God. The call to the cloister is also bedeviled by Pharisaism, in which one falls into the delusion that one is making oneself morally acceptable to God and therefore superior to the ordinary Christian. Closely related are the pitfalls of legalism, where monastic works are made a condition for salvation, and of rigorism, in which strictness of living is deemed necessary to arrive at life's spiritual goal.[34]

Likewise, Bloesch writes in an unpublished theological notebook that "two things have made me question (but not deny) the validity of the monastic vocation. The first is the legalism that I observed in the Anglo-Catholic monasteries I studied while in Oxford." Bloesch's hesitation in supporting monasticism when it seems to teach that one's salvation is earned through works grows out of his soteriology. Bloesch believes that a holy life is not a prerequisite for our salvation, much less is it our salvation. Rather, a holy life is a sign and is the evidence of the authenticity of our salvation. As he

---

34. Bloesch, *Struggle of Prayer*, 144.

writes in his work on Christology, "Sanctification is not simply a consequence or effect of justification but the crown and goal of justification."[35] Bloesch holds to a Reformed soteriology, which teaches (1) that by God's redemption, the Christian is delivered from his/her slavery to sin; (2) that by propitiation, God's wrath against sin is turned away from the believer; (3) that atonement for sin occurred once for all in the life and death of Jesus Christ; (4) that the believer is reconciled to God; (5) that believers are regenerated by the inward cleansing of the Holy Spirit; and (6) that God imputes his perfect righteousness to all who believe in Jesus Christ. The central salvific act, for Bloesch, is justification, where "God declares the sinner righteous by virtue of faith in the perfect holiness of Jesus Christ, thereby restoring the sinner to the positive favor of God."[36] With the magisterial reformers, Bloesch believes that one's salvation is due solely to the free, unmerited grace of God. Whereas for Protestants in general, one's redemption is wrought by Christ alone without our aid or cooperation, Roman Catholics, Bloesch writes, believe that Christians do, in fact, cooperate in their own salvation: "The gulf between Reformation theology and Roman Catholic theology revolves around this issue: Is our salvation a cooperative endeavor in which we are assisted by grace in preparing the way for justification, or is our salvation an act accomplished by Christ alone (*solus Christus*) whose benefits are then applied to us by the Spirit?"[37] Having stated that Roman Catholic (and Eastern Orthodox) theologians teach that salvation is by grace *and* works, Bloesch concludes his treatment by insisting that justification is by grace alone. Returning to the issue of the Anglo-Catholic monasticism that Bloesch was exposed to during his postdoctoral work in Oxford, he perceived a kind of works-righteousness in these communities—that is, that they believed that their monastic lifestyle was somehow salvific, since they were cooperating with God in their salvation. This is the same critique that Martin Luther and John Calvin leveled against monasticism, writes Bloesch:

> Both Luther and Calvin declared themselves opposed to monasticism as it then existed in the Roman Catholic Church. Their principal criticism was that the monastic life was seen to be more meritorious than ordinary Christian living. Monastic spirituality was actually a type of works-righteousness that stood in

---

35. Bloesch, *Jesus Christ*, 182.
36. Ibid., 177.
37. Ibid., 179.

contradiction to the evangelical message of justification by free grace.[38]

Such a view of monasticism, which was salvifically and spiritually superior to an "ordinary" Christian life, also caused Bloesch to suggest that monasticism was prone towards an unchristian "mysticism" as well as pharisaism.

Bloesch has always been leery of what he terms "mysticism," which he often discusses. He believes that "Christian mysticism as a movement and tradition has diverged from the biblical witness by making this element the criterion and ground of Christian thinking." Instead of being a means to holiness, mysticism has become the end in itself. For Bloesch, "Evangelical spirituality is a spirituality of compassion rather than of contemplation. It is oriented about the self-sacrificial love that descends to the undeserving rather than the unitive love that ascends to infinite being." Because the Scriptures command the believer to love God and to love one's neighbor, any spirituality that advocates a mystical experience over service to one's neighbor is to be rejected. In *The Struggle of Prayer*, Bloesch writes that the "eremitic and monastic ways are constantly threatened by a false kind of mysticism in which one's attention is turned away from the anguish of the world to the vision of God."[39] This is an error because "in biblical spirituality asceticism involves disciplines that equip us for ministry. In mystical religion asceticism is valued as a way of insuring salvation." This form of mysticism, Bloesch believes, leads to an erroneous soteriology, one in which justification of sin is limited to and directly connected with one's level of righteousness and holiness. Instead of holding that justification is an imputation of righteousness, as those in the Reformed tradition believe, mystics, writes Bloesch, "see justification as being realized in the birth of God in the soul."[40] In a personal interview with me, Bloesch stated that Pelagianism and semi-Pelagianism are also characteristic of much "older monasticism" and that those in the Reformed tradition are unable to incorporate themselves into current Roman Catholic and Eastern Orthodox monastic communities because of these soteriological differences. This is a theme that he has pursued elsewhere in his writings, especially in those that are concerned with a theology of the church. As we have already seen, in one text he goes so far as to say that the sixteenth-century reformers were primarily against the monastic orders not because they were dismis-

38. Bloesch, *Wellsprings of Renewal*, 29.
39. Bloesch, *Struggle of Prayer*, 144.
40. Bloesch, *Crisis of Piety*, 105–6.

sive of community life per se, but rather because of the theology of works-righteousness that these orders espoused or, at least, appeared to espouse. Further, Bloesch believes that mysticism has an ahistorical orientation, in that the Son in the soul is more important than the historical incarnation of Jesus Christ and that mysticism seeks after an impersonal God. This ultimately leads to a kind of soteriological dualism, that a person must perform good works in order to make God's grace operative in one's life. For Bloesch, this simply results in an obscuring of the biblical emphasis on grace "by a synergistic orientation."[41]

Another of Bloesch's concerns is that life in the cloister can lead to what he terms pharisaism, ghettoism, or archaism—that is, a perceived superiority of the monastic life over the life of the "ordinary" Christian. With Martin Luther and other reformers, he thinks that it would be wrong to say that he is interested in restoring religious life, since all of one's life is religious life. Bloesch has consistently held this position. He writes in one of this theological notebooks that "those who embrace a monastic life are not necessarily to be regarded as exceptional saints. To be sure, they have chosen an exceptional or extraordinary vocation. Yet only a very few of these actually become in themselves extra-ordinary Christians." Likewise, a "Protestant religious community will not see itself as an ideal society or utopia. . . . Neither will it regard its way of life as higher or superior to the common life. . . . Rather, it will view itself as a practical form of service to Christ—neither superior nor inferior to other modes of service, but nevertheless legitimate." In *The Future of Evangelical Christianity*, he refers to this as "the double standard of [Roman] Catholic spirituality," where one group of Christians is to live under the vows of celibacy, poverty, and obedience, while all other Christians are merely "ordinary believers."[42]

Bloesch's other concern is that monasticism tends toward rigorism and legalism. In his volume dedicated to ecclesiology, Bloesch writes, "I have detected snares in community life including . . . legalism, in which law supplants gospel as the motivating force and criterion for Christian living."[43] Elsewhere, he defines legalism as that attitude in which a person thinks that their monastic works are a condition for salvation and where one's rigorous living is judged to be necessary to arrive at the spiritual goal of holiness. One way to avoid this snare, writes Bloesch, is for a community

---

41. Bloesch, *Wellsprings of Renewal*, 30.
42. Bloesch, *Future of Evangelical Christianity*, 114.
43. Bloesch, *Church*, 214.

Donald Bloesch and the Evangelical Tradition

to continually place its salvific confidence in the free offer of God's grace. That is, instead of relying upon themselves to keep the letter of the law, the community members should always look to the finished work of Jesus Christ on the cross, realizing that salvation is found there and only there. He goes on to say in *The Church* that an "evangelical community will be constantly alert to the dangers of legalism and self-righteousness that elevate community life to a higher level spiritually than ordinary life in the world. In evangelical theology all Christians are under the gospel imperative of wholehearted consecration to Christ. . . . Having done all, they will continue to confess that they are only sinners saved by grace, that faith alone secures their salvation and that Christ alone is to be given all glory in the procuring of their salvation."[44]

In short, Bloesch's concerns center around three important tensions: (1) substituting a mystical-based soteriology for that of the Reformed perspective (as understood by Bloesch); (2) falsely creating a spiritual dichotomy between those who enter the monastic life and those living a non-monastic Christian life; and (3) mistaking the nature of the monastic life to somehow be more salvific than God's offer of free grace extended to all believers. In reaction to these perceived understandings, Bloesch has attempted to craft a theology of the monastic life that would avoid these tendencies, whether real or perceived.

Donald Bloesch understands that religious communities and religious orders have a long history in the Christian tradition. He also understands that the rise of Protestant monasteries and religious communities soon after the Reformation of the sixteenth century was the result of "the deep-felt yearning in the human spirit for the kind of consecration the monasteries had symbolized [in the past]," coupled with the fact that the existence of monasteries "could not long remain stifled."[45] For Bloesch, the Reformers made a mistake by eliminating monasteries: "The Reformation, in its reaction to perversions and misunderstandings of biblical truth in the popular [Roman] Catholic piety of the time, regrettably discarded much in the catholic heritage that is of enduring value. I have in mind such things as religious orders within the church, celibacy, retreats and spiritual disciplines, including meditation and silence."[46] Even Pietists, Bloesch rightly insists, saw the need for times of periodic solitude. In addition, Bloesch holds that

---

44. Bloesch, *Church*, 215.
45. Bloesch, *Wellsprings of Renewal*, 35.
46. Bloesch, *Future of Evangelical Christianity*, 133.

there are three types of discipleship in the Christian Scriptures and in traditional Christian spirituality. The first is the active life—that is, pursuing a secular vocation outside of the church; the second is the contemplative or monastic life; and the third type is a mixed life—that is, when one leads a religious life outside of the cloister, similar to the medieval mendicant friars or congregations of priests. In his *Wellsprings of Renewal*, Bloesch presents more simply this tripartite division as two patterns of discipleship: those who are called to live in the world for the sake of the gospel, and others who "stand under the imperative to fulfill their vocation apart from the world in religious communities or in solitary witness that often entails the renunciation of family, property, and the use of force or violence."[47] Simply put, Bloesch refers to these two patterns of life as the secular life and the religious life. Instead of pitting these two patterns against one another, Bloesch says that they are complementary, that the church needs both, since both involve inward separation from the things of the world as well as inward sacrifice.

Taken together, these thoughts suggest that, in many ways, Bloesch implicitly recognizes the historical existence of the institution of monasticism and simply expects that such an institution should exist in the evangelical church to which he addresses himself. In one of his most recent theological notebooks, he even affirms that in "our controversy with Rome we as evangelicals tend to forget that the Protestant Reformation was born in a monastery." He goes further, however, by providing some subtle theological support for the institution of monasticism as well. He writes that "monasticism at its best, however, reminds us that no sacrifice is too great for the one who is serious about Christian commitment and that the fellowship of sacrificial love that transcends the claims of home and family can be realized in part now as a sign and parable of the coming eschatological kingdom."[48] Bloesch also views monasticism as more of a genuine spiritual movement of renewal, as opposed to an ideological movement that is only interested in serving the interests of a particular party. This being the case, monasticism serves to expand the kingdom of God, since this is the primary purpose of any authentic spiritual movement. How then, according to Bloesch, does monasticism help to expand the kingdom of God? What role(s) do monasteries perform in the church? Bloesch's answers to these questions fall easily into three categories: monasteries as training centers, monasteries

47. Bloesch, *Wellsprings of Renewal*, 20.
48. Bloesch, *Struggle of Prayer*, 144.

as centers of evangelism, and monasteries as critics and correctors of the larger church.

In his *Future of Evangelical Christianity*, Bloesch writes that "in evangelical perspective, a monastery will function as a training center for mission rather than a testing ground to prepare oneself for heaven. Its goal will be not the ascent of divinity but the apostolate to the nations."[49] Bloesch makes a nearly identical statement about monasteries being an apostolate to the nations in his theological notebook from the same period: the "kind of monastery that I uphold is one that is imbued with the prophetic spirituality of biblical faith rather than the mystical spirituality of monistic religion. Such a monastery has as its goal not the ascent to divinity but the apostolate to the nations." What exactly it means for a monastery to be a training center "for mission" is unclear, though Bloesch believes that this is the role that Martin Luther envisioned for Protestant monasticism. Bloesch hints at an answer in an entry of his theological notebook. Here we read that a strictly "monastic community . . . is designed to help one find God in the solitariness of the cloister," whereas an "evangelical community . . . functions as a training center for mission." From this dichotomy, we can conclude that the "mission" envisioned by Bloesch is not that of living a solitary life, perhaps not even one wholly dedicated to a life of prayer for self, others, and the world. Thus, for Bloesch, it seems that the heart of an evangelical religious community would not be grounded in an acquisition of holiness, but on availability of service, though the two are not necessarily mutually exclusive. Bloesch's best example of this combination of pursuit of holiness and availability of service is the previously mentioned Ecumenical Sisterhood of Mary as presented in his *Centers of Christian Renewal* and which continues today as the Ecumenical Community of the Sisters of Mary. The sisterhood was (and is) dedicated to prayer and evangelism. In its earliest days, the sisters were markedly contemplative, evidenced by the infrequency with which the sisters left the monastery, as well as by their keeping of the sevenfold canonical office of hours. Furthermore, there was a strong theology of the bridal love of Christ—that is, the sisters saw themselves as brides of Christ and sought to cultivate a very personal and intimate communion with Christ. Yet, the community was also fixed upon the task of evangelism: "The sisters actively seek for the conversion of the lost through prayer, proclamation (by the written as well as the spoken word),

---

49. Bloesch, *Future of Evangelical Christianity*, 144.

Reforming the Monastery

and spiritual counsel (which is given to the many guests and visitors)."[50] Perhaps these monastic training centers, like the Ecumenical Sisterhood of Mary, would dedicate themselves to equipping others for the task of evangelism. This coheres well with Bloesch's second category of monasteries as centers of evangelism.

In addition to holding doctrinal theology in balance with a theology of the spiritual life, Donald Bloesch also believes that one must couple a theology of the spiritual life with a theology of evangelism. It is likely this belief that leads him to connect his understanding of evangelical monasticism with the responsibility of these monasteries to be centers of evangelism, though he is not unaware of the historical role that monasteries served in the task of evangelism. In one of his earliest writings, *The Crisis of Piety*, Bloesch writes that the evangelical monasteries that he imagines "would be analogous to the Catholic monasteries of the middle ages, functioning as lighthouses to the churches as well as to a lost and dying world."[51] This understanding of monasteries as centers of evangelism continue to echo throughout his later, more mature writings as well. In an unpublished theological notebook, he asserts that an evangelical monastery would not motivate itself so much by a search for God or by a need to encounter some sort of "other," but rather "by the desire to glorify God by witnessing to Christ, by sharing the gospel of what God has done for us in Christ." Similarly, also in an unpublished theological notebook, he writes that "as evangelical Christians we seek not the replication of the monastic ideal but a new kind of fellowship whose accent is not withdrawal from the world but the permeation of the world with the gospel." In the same notebook, Bloesch also writes that the "goal of an evangelical monasticism is not the purification and redemption of the seeker after truth but the dissemination of the gospel in a new way and time." What this actually looks like in practice is conditional on Bloesch's own understanding of evangelism. In Bloesch's estimation, the real problem in the task of evangelism is not just that people lack knowledge of the gospel, but that they actively lack the will to believe. Therefore, for effective evangelism, one must rely on the regenerating work of the Holy Spirit. An evangelist presents the gospel by way of kerygmatic proclamation, coupled with fervent prayer and deeds of love. Bloesch writes that this is the approach that does not appeal to some sort of a common ground with those who hear the gospel, but to the sovereign grace of

---

50. Bloesch, *Centers of Christian Renewal*, 117.
51. Bloesch, *Crisis of Piety*, xi.

God. Who better to devote themselves to the task of preaching the gospel, praying for the lost, and deeds of love than those joined to a monastery?

Not only does Bloesch give monasteries the role of evangelizing the unconverted, he also envisions that evangelical Protestant monasteries will serve as leaven to those already converted to the Christian faith. In one theological notebook, he writes that such a role for monasteries flows naturally out of his understanding that the "parsonage, when it is not related to the cloister, is in danger of accommodation to the world." As well, for Bloesch, Protestant religious communities should be discerning critics of the church, not merely an obedient servant to the church. Monasteries could correct the wrongs within the church and not simply be complicit in these wrongs themselves. "We need not a return to the monastery," he writes, "but a new penetration of the gospel into the darkness of the secular world that will include the monastic vision of a company of men and women wholly dedicated to God. Ideally the local church should exemplify this vision, but there are times when local congregations need to be backed up by special working fellowships that signify not a higher way in the vocation of discipleship but a different way." There seems to be an implicit critique of the church here, in that the need for a monastery seems to be dependent on some lack in the institutional church itself. Yet, regardless of any weakness in the church's own execution of its mission, Bloesch still posits a place for the monastery to act as a partner, supporter, and critic: "... contemplative vocations may be more necessary even than those which unite prayer and service in the world. The church, including the evangelical church, ever needs the monastery as a sign of God's new order that stands over against the powers and structures of the world."[52] In short, the church needs the monastery.

Between 1992 and 2004, Bloesch published his seven-volume magnum opus, the Christian Foundations series. In the volume dedicated to ecclesiology, Bloesch devotes significant space to discussing the institution of monasticism. In this volume, he presents his most synthetic and mature offering on the nature and role of evangelical monasticism, which is worth quoting at length. He writes,

> I sincerely welcome the new surge in community life, but I wish to enumerate some guiding principles for those contemplating this kind of vocation. First, the paradigm for evangelical community life should be the natural family. . . . An evangelical community

52. Bloesch, *Struggle of Prayer*, 152 n. 36.

will try to combine the first, second and third orders of Catholic tradition so that married and single work together to prepare the way for the coming of the kingdom of God. . . . Second, an evangelical community will be based solidly on the biblical message of justification by the free grace of God. The monastic life is not a means by which we earn justification for ourselves, but a sign that justification has already been accomplished through the atoning death and glorious resurrection of our Lord Jesus Christ. . . . Third, a community in the evangelical sense will be a center for evangelism and world mission. It will be both a training center for mission and a locus of mission. . . . The certification of a community as evangelical will be based not on how well it keeps the canonical hours but on the significance it attaches to the proclamation of faith in the main service of worship. Such a community will also be measured by the depth of its prayers for the church and the world, its fidelity to the Bible in its preaching and teaching ministry and its generosity in offering hospitality. Fourth, the community will be solidly grounded in private and corporate prayer including adoration, confession, thanksgiving and petition. . . . The evangelical communalist will be devoted to intercession for the world rather than to the perfection and transfiguration of the seeking soul. . . . Again, an evangelical community will not claim to be an embodiment of the kingdom of God, nor will it set out to build the kingdom of God on earth (as in utopian communities). Instead, it will endeavor to be a sign and witness of the kingdom, whose coming is in the hands of the living God. The community will see itself standing under the judgment of the kingdom and therefore will be open to continual reform and purification by the Spirit of God. Finally, the evangelical community will be intimately related to the evangelical church. . . . In evangelical parlance it is more appropriate to speak of interdenominational fellowships of renewal rather than of monastic orders, since the accent is not on separation and withdrawal but on the penetration of society with the values and goals of Christian faith. The purpose is not to sunder the lines of communication with the wider church but to make an impact on the church through word and life and thereby contribute to its revitalization. The community must sound the call to periodic withdrawal from the tempests of the world but withdrawal only for the sake of return, this time on a deeper level.[53]

Here we see Bloesch reiterating his consistent thinking regarding monasticism in the evangelical church: (1) evangelical monasticism is based on a

53. Bloesch, *Church*, 214-17.

Donald Bloesch and the Evangelical Tradition

theology of justification by God alone; (2) an evangelical monastery will be a center for evangelism throughout the world; and (3) the evangelical monastic community will be intimately connected to the evangelical church and will serve as its critic and, by extension, its source of renewal. Bloesch also iterates here the obvious and historical understanding of the monastery as a center of prayer. Finally, he lays out clearly his understanding that the paradigm for monastic life in the evangelical church is the family. This is likely rooted in Bloesch's erroneous belief that ancient Christian monks and nuns embraced asceticism primarily in order to curb physical lust. Thus, marriage moves the agent of curbing lust from the monastery to the marriage relationship, presumably freeing up the (married) monastic to devote himself more fully to his apostolates of praying, training, evangelizing, and/or serving as critic and corrector in the church. Bloesch expands on this understanding when he writes in an unpublished theological notebook that in "traditional Roman Catholic spirituality,"

> the sexual drive is regarded as an obstacle to Christian service, and therefore abstinence is strongly recommended if not required for those who wish to enter into full-time service for Christ and his kingdom. In evangelical spirituality, the sexual drive always poses a threat to Christian service, but it can at the same time be an aid in such service when it serves to bring man and woman together as covenant partners in the intimacy of married love. For evangelicals, the loneliness of celibacy can also be an obstacle to kingdom service, even while it may offer the freedom to pursue special kinds of ministry that marriage might disallow or make exceedingly difficult.

Regardless of the accuracy of Bloesch's understanding of both monastic history and Roman Catholicism, it is clear that he sees both celibacy and the married life as being viable options for those entering an evangelical monastic life. This tension between celibacy and the married life and their influence on one's ministry goes back to Bloesch's earliest publications as well. In *The Christian Life and Salvation* (1967), Bloesch insists that

> the counsel to celibacy as given in Matthew 19:10–12 must also not be regarded as referring to a more perfect or higher way of salvation. This counsel can be accepted by those who discern in celibacy a more practical way of serving Christ in the situation in which they find themselves. There is certainly a place for the witness of those who espouse poverty and celibacy for the sake of Christian mission, and Protestantism on the whole neglected this

way of service to its detriment. The present revival of community life in Protestantism is to be welcomed in that it reminds us that discipleship exists not only in the world but also apart from and against the world. Yet those who renounce the world outwardly are not to be regarded as more worthy or holy in the sight of God than those who bear their cross in the midst of home and family. Indeed, marriage and family, when grounded in Christ, can be regarded as particular modes of cross-bearing which certainly serve to strengthen faith and advance the cause of the kingdom.[54]

Again, it is important to state that Bloesch is not rejecting celibacy; rather, he is attempting to create a space for those who have chosen marriage to respond also to a call to the monastic life. Bloesch puts it simply in one of his theological notebooks: "Christian life should ideally be a balance between solitude and fellowship. We need solitude in order to be alone with God in prayer and to reflect on the vocation that God has given us. But we also need fellowship in order to sustain us in the struggle to live out our vocation in the world." One finds such fellowship, for Bloesch, through the institutions of marriage and monasticism.

As the current work demonstrates, Donald Bloesch is not the first Reformed Christian theologian to develop a theology of the monastic life. Bloesch is distinctive, however, in that he directs his writings and theology in general toward the English-speaking North American evangelical church. This will likely give him an audience that even Karl Barth has not greatly influenced outside of the academy. For those in this tradition who resolve to take Bloesch's theology of the monastic life seriously, it is time to see monasteries arise as an evangelizing, educational, and edificatory institution. It is time to see the institution of monasticism serve the spiritual needs of those evangelicals who recognize, like Bloesch, that one's salvation and one's Christian life are intimately connected. Thus, for its salvation, the evangelical church to which Donald Bloesch addresses himself must reintroduce the monastic life and has begun to do so.

Protestant Calls for Monasticism

In 1979, Peter Monkres, a pastor in the United Church of Christ, wrote that the mainline Protestant churches in North America needed to reintroduce monasticism in order to the give surplus clergy—that is, those unable to

---

54. Bloesch, *Christian Life and Salvation*, 81.

find work in shrinking mainline churches—an opportunity to fulfill their ministerial calling. Monkres rightly notes that such an excess of clergy could and certainly should be "an antidote for the harassment and helplessness which poison life's experience." In fact, he writes,

> One possibility for achieving this goal is by creating networks of religious communities—a new monastic order for ministers and their families who either cannot find parishes or who seek alternatives to traditional forms of parish ministry. Such a community would be a core or center within which to undertake a silent search for God in meditation, prayer and liturgy, or from which to go into the world to do the deeds of healing. The thrust of each community would be determined by those persons who feel called to it to develop the discipline of common life and common witness.[55]

Monkres goes on to describe these proposed monastic communities as centers that would offer alternatives to the normal consumerist patterns of Western culture, as places for spiritual renewal for both pastors and laity, and as potential centers of ongoing intellectual and spiritual formation. In the following year, *The Christian Century* published another call to Protestants to reintroduce monasticism into its ranks. James Baker, a Southern Baptist professor at Western Kentucky University, wrote that "Protestantism is not necessarily antimystical, but it has always been antimonastic.... Every church needs bishops, preachers, counselors, scholars and monks. Protestants, most of us, have all but the last of these, and in their absence could lie the key to one of our most debilitating deficiencies: our spiritual witness." He goes on to describe that, despite being birthed by monks, Protestantism soon dismissed its monastic heritage, labeling it "Catholic" or "popish," something to be avoided and shunned. Moreover, writes Baker, Protestants are certainly not interested in the three qualities that define monasticism: poverty, obedience, and chastity. This leaves us with a "chronic Protestant spiritual deficiency," that we are not an "authentically prayerful people."[56] Thus, Protestants need a form of monasticism that will restore this lost dimension of spirituality, says Baker.

Nearly a decade later, in 1988, an editorial appeared in *Christianity Today*, the flagship periodical of evangelicalism, with the title "Remonking the Church." This editorial, much like the articles by Monkres and

---

55. Monkres, "Innovative Ministry for Surplus Clergy," 148.
56. Baker, "Benedict's Children and Their Separated Brothers and Sisters," 1192–93.

Reforming the Monastery

Baker, spends some time talking about the vices of the contemporary church. According to the editorial's author, Rodney Clapp, the evangelical church is infected by violence, sensuality, and materialism. Although it stands against the culture, the evangelical church finds itself adopting softer versions of the larger culture. To counteract this tendency, writes Clapp, the evangelical church needs to engage in a process of remonasticization. Clapp explains the process:

> The remonasticization we would support would not be as tightly defined as traditional monasticism. It would not, for example, mean the stereotypical cluster of people retiring to desert solitude. Rather, it would look to the biblical antecedents for a select group of holy persons set apart to call all persons to holiness, such as the Old Testament Nazirites, Israel's witness as a light to all nations, and Jesus' calling of disciples to train and teach with the goal of drawing all Israel to the same discipleship. And, of course, there is the church itself—which is supposed to be no more than it hopes the world will someday be. In this context, remonasticization might take several forms, all oriented towards service in and to the world.

Unmarried believers would live together in community, witnessing together against violence, materialism, and a sinful sexuality. Families could purchase multiple homes in the same neighborhood so that they could meet daily for common worship and mutual discipleship. Older Christians entering into their retirement years might form communities that devote time to worship, biblical study, and service in the world. Clapp concludes the editorial by identifying two practices as central for evangelical monks: 1) "they must learn and then teach others how to live our world into line with that of the Bible"; and 2) evangelical monks "must recover the life of prayer."[57] Though Monkres', Baker's, and Clapp's calls are not directly responsible for the emergence of the New monasticism, in spirit it is largely sympathetic to what each of them proposed.

According to Rob Moll, the birth of the new monastic movement occurred at a June 2004 conference held in Durham, North Carolina.[58] At this conference, sixty practitioners of the new monasticism, as well as academics, gathered together to give shape to an emerging movement that was, at the time, comprised of a number of disparate and unrelated individuals

57. Clapp, "Remonking the Church," 20–21.
58. Moll, "New Monasticism," 40.

Donald Bloesch and the Evangelical Tradition

and intentional communities. At the conference, the twelve marks of new monasticism were discussed and elaborated upon:

1) Relocation to the abandoned places of Empire.

2) Sharing economic resources with fellow community members and the needy among us.

3) Hospitality to the stranger.

4) Lament for racial divisions within the church and our communities combined with the active pursuit of a just reconciliation.

5) Humble submission to Christ's body, the church.

6) Intentional formation in the way of Christ and the rule of the community along the lines of the old novitiate.

7) Nurturing common life among members of intentional community.

8) Support for celibate singles alongside monogamous married couples and their children.

9) Geographical proximity to community members who share a common rule of life.

10) Care for the plot of God's earth given to us along with support of our local economies.

11) Peacemaking in the midst of violence and conflict resolution within communities along the lines of Matthew 18.

12) Commitment to a disciplined contemplative life.[59]

Since 2004, an unknown number of communities have identified themselves with the new monastic movement, living according to the twelve marks. Though there is not one particular rule of life for all of these communities, the twelve marks bring these communities into a kind of monastic order. Due to the disparity of practices in these new monastic communities, it is impossible to describe all of them easily, but living simply in community, working on behalf of the disadvantaged and the poor, and building relationships in specific neighborhoods are all central to the new monastics. According to Jonathan Wilson-Hartgrove, however, the new monastics are really not all that new, and it is important that they see themselves as

---

59. See the volume edited by members of The Rutba House, *School(s) for Conversion*, xii–xiii.

belonging within the larger monastic history, including Protestant monastic history.[60]

Similar in inspiration to the new monastic movement is the "New Friars" movement, described most eloquently by Scott Bessenecker. What he says about the new friars can also be said about the new monastics: "This emerging, missional renewal movement has been inspired by the ancient wisdom of the historic orders. They exist on the outer edge of the mainstream church like the historic orders, and they enjoy many of the disciplines and liturgies developed within the historic orders."[61] These new friars, like the new monastics, are a disparate group that takes their inspiration from the mendicant orders of the medieval and modern church, such as the Franciscans and Dominicans. Given that friars are historically known for their poverty, the new friars often work in the slums and other poor areas of major metropolitan centers around the world. Again, both the new monastics and the new friars are responding to the call for the remonking of the evangelical church, but there still appears to be room for a more traditional, contemplative form of monasticism in the evangelical church.

William Carey

An historical precedent for a more traditional form of monasticism can be found in the life of William Carey and his mission establishment of Serampore. Born in 1761, William Carey was apprenticed to a shoemaker at fourteen years old, but acknowledged a call to ministry before the age of twenty. At twenty-four, he took over the pastoral responsibilities for a dissenting congregation in Moulton, England, where he met Andrew Fuller, a Baptist minister and his eventual lifelong partner in missionary activity. At Moulton, Carey became a schoolteacher, becoming enthralled with James Cooke's voyages around the world. At this time Carey took an interest in the "moral and spiritual degradation of the heathen," and the idea of a mission to the "heathen" began to take shape in Carey's imagination.[62]

At the age of twenty-eight, Carey moved to a pastorate in Leicester, preaching in May 1792 his great sermon in which he admonished his hearers to expect great things from God and to attempt great things for God.

60. Wilson-Hartgrove, *New Monasticism*.
61. Bessenecker, *Living Mission*, 21.
62. Marshman, *Life and Times of Carey, Marshman, and Ward*, 1:9.

Donald Bloesch and the Evangelical Tradition

The result of this sermon was the foundations for a society for propagating the gospel among the heathen, setting up the Baptist Missionary Union. Though gathering little domestic support, the agency, having received a request from Bengal to make their presence known there, chose India as the destination of their first missionaries. In June 1793, Carey and his family set sail for India, setting up a base in Malda the following year. By 1797, Carey had translated the New Testament into Bengali, had contracted with the government to establish an indigo farm, and was ready to welcome new missionaries from the Society. In response, the Society sent William Ward and Joshua Marshman; together the three missionaries established the Serampore Mission.

Serampore was a small Danish town sixteen miles upriver from Calcutta. Upon declaring their intentions of setting up a mission center from which to evangelize, they were asked by the British authorities to desist from their intentions. The British viewed missionary work as an interference in its goal of establishing industries in India. In response, the Danish invited them to stay, assuring them of the protection of the Danish government. They were offered Danish passports so that they could travel easily through land owned by the British and were offered the church being constructed by the Danish. After careful consideration, though with some reluctance, Carey decided to leave the Malda district and create a settlement at Serampore. The original plan was to establish a mission on the plan of a Moravian settlement—that is, communities that placed special focus on prayer and worship, simplicity of lifestyle, and distribution of financial resources. These communities existed to aid in the sanctification of its members and to create an environment in which to raise up supporters of Moravian mission work around the world. Carey and his associates, in setting up Serampore, agreed to hold all things in common, dine at a common table, and to give each family a small allowance for personal expenditures. Like the Moravian settlements, all residents of Serampore were considered equal and were expected to lead devotions and preach in turn. The oversight of the community was entrusted to each missionary in a monthly rotation. A house was purchased and held in trust by each of the missionaries and a printing press, purchased by Carey, was set up to print the New Testament in Bengali, as well as gospel tracts and religious pamphlets. On May 1, 1800, Joshua Marshman and his wife opened two boarding schools on the property to assist in the support of the mission.

Reforming the Monastery

These schools became the main economic means by which the community was able to remain in existence.

According to missiologist Ralph Winter, the Serampore Brotherhood was a "task-oriented community that approximated a Roman Catholic order."[63] He goes on to acknowledge in a footnote, however, that the "parallel is a bit difficult," due to the fact that the Serampore community remained a local fellowship, whereas most Roman Catholic religious orders grew to be worldwide organizations. Regardless, Carey appears to have envisioned that his community would take the form of a religious order. Already in 1792, in his *Enquiry*, Carey had developed his ideas of a missionary community. In a section of the *Enquiry* titled "An Enquiry into the Duty of Christians in general, and what Means ought to be used, in order to promote this Work," Carey writes,

> Suppose a company of serious Christians, ministers and private persons, were to form themselves into a society, and make a number of rules respecting the regulation of the plan, and the persons who are to be employed as missionaries, the means of defraying the expense, &c. &c. This society must consist of persons whose hearts are in the work, men of serious religion, and possessing a spirit of perseverance; there must be a determination not to admit any person who is not of this description, or to retain him longer than he answers to it.[64]

Though Carey imagined that his company would originate from his own Baptist denomination, he goes on to say that he does not imagine that its membership would be limited to any particular denomination: "I wish with all my heart, that everyone who loves our Lord Jesus Christ in sincerity, would in some way or other engage in it." It is more expedient, Carey believes, for the company to be denominationally specific, since this would reduce the number of discords that would arise from various denominations working together. The rich and those of more moderate income would support this company. Carey believes that if the rich and those of moderate income gave a tithe of their income, then it would be possible to support both domestic and international missions. It would appear that the Serampore Mission was the kind of community that Carey had envisioned in the *Enquiry*.

---

63. Winter, "William Carey's Major Novelty," 203.
64. Carey, *Enquiry*, 82.

Donald Bloesch and the Evangelical Tradition

It is likely that Carey may have been familiar with Roman Catholic mission work through Robert Millar's *History of the Propagation of Christianity, and Overthrow of Paganism*, published in 1723. Christopher Smith says that Carey "had surely read" this work and would have been able to learn from the stories of José de Acosta, Francis Xavier, Roberto de Nobili, and other Jesuit missionaries.[65] Thus, Winter concludes that Carey had learned about the structure of Roman Catholic religious orders and it was this structure which was the impetus for his foundation at Serampore. This would make the Serampore Mission a kind of Protestant religious order. Regarding the Serampore Mission's similarity to and dependence on Moravian settlements, Winter notes that "the only structural pattern available to Carey was that of the Moravian missions, to which the Serampore Brotherhood was, indeed, very similar and to which Carey and the others often made reference. However, the Moravian pattern was, in turn, very similar to that of the Benedictines." He concludes, "We are suggesting a functional similarity, not a direct connection, between the Serampore Brotherhood and any particular Roman order."[66] Winter acknowledges that Protestants rejected the structural vehicle of Roman Catholic orders simply because they rejected Roman Catholicism writ large. Carey, in the *Enquiry*, however, had advocated a kind of religious order, suggesting that the Serampore Mission was a parallel to such Roman Catholic structures. For example, the Serampore Brotherhood lived by a "Form of Agreement" that, in many ways, paralleled a Roman Catholic religious rule of life. Like most religious rules, it was legislated that the document would be read aloud to the community, in this case on the first Sunday of January, May, and October. The Serampore document was enacted by the community on October 7, 1805, and contains eleven principles meant to govern the life of the community.

First, the community sets "an infinite value upon immortal souls" by fixing its mind on the "awful doctrine of eternal punishment." By doing so, the members of the community are most able to engage in the shared task of evangelizing the lost. Instead of despairing that the work is too difficult or that the Indian people are too engrossed in their worship of false gods, members of the Serampore community trusted in God to purify the hearts of those to whom they ministered, putting aside forever "their idols to the moles and to the bats."[67]

65. Smith, "Tale of Many Models," 487.
66. Winter, "William Carey's Major Novelty," 207.
67. Oussoren, *William Carey*, 274–75. Hereafter cited parenthetically by page number.

Second, the community commits to learn all that it can about the philosophy and life of those to whom it intends to minister, so that it "shall be able to converse with them in an intelligible manner." The community seeks to know "their modes of thinking, their habits, their propensities, their antipathies, the way in which they reason about God, sin, holiness, the way of salvation," and their manner and method of worshipping; thus the community can know how best to evangelize them. The community commits to gathering this knowledge through direct conversation, reading their published works, and "attentively observing their manners and customs" (275). Results of this commitment to learning the native languages and culture resulted in such publications as Carey's *Grammar of the Mahratta Language* (1805) and his *Dictionary of the Mahratta Language* (1810), as well as William Ward's *View of the History, Literature, and Mythology of the Hindoos: including a minute description of their manners and customs, and translations from their principal works* (1815).

Third, members of the community commit to "abstain from those things which would increase [the Hindus] prejudices against the Gospel" (275). This includes keeping English customs out of the public eye, avoiding cruelty to animals, not dwelling on the sins of the Hindu gods, and not harming their images or interrupting their worship. The community saw an example for this approach in the life of the Apostle Paul, who strove to become all things to all people (cf. 1 Cor 9:19–23), as well as in the pattern established by the Moravians and the Quakers in ministering to the Native American Indians.

Fourth, the community takes advantage of all opportunities for doing good to the Indians. Despite the excessively warm climate, the community agreed to take every opportunity to speak to those among whom they ministered, by preaching, visiting villages and markets, and talking to anyone, despite their caste, as the opportunity arose.

Fifth, the community's preaching would be centered on Christ crucified, for the "doctrine of Christ's expiatory death and all-sufficient merits had been, and must ever remain, the great means of conversion." This doctrine is seen to have been a constant source of nourishment and sanctification for the church, therefore it must be preached by the Serampore missionaries. Interestingly, the document asserts that it was the preaching of this doctrine in particular which caused the Reformation to spread with such rapidity. Moreover, this doctrine was also held by the Puritans and was preached by the more modern evangelists, including John Wesley and

George Whitefield. Further, "it is a well-known fact that the most successful missionaries in the world at the present day make the atonement of Christ their continued theme. We mean the Moravians" (277).

Sixth, the community would do all in their power to make the native Indians feel at home in their company. This would be gained by listening to their complaints, giving them kind advice, and making community decisions openly. The community would give the Indians free access to them and treat them as equals. In this manner, the document says, no sacrifice is too great since the salvation of souls is at stake.

Seventh, the community committed to catechizing the Indians slowly, so that they learn well the truths of the Christian faith, thereby establishing them firmly in the faith. Also, the community will assist converts in finding employment, since conversion to Christianity will likely have cost them their jobs and connections of support with their families. Not to do this would cause the community to "be guilty of great cruelty." Simply put, the brotherhood affirms that it would disciple those Indians who came to faith in Christ:

> To bear the faults of our native brethren, so as to reprove them with tenderness, and set them right in the necessity of a holy conversation, is a very necessary duty. We should remember the gross darkness in which they were so lately involved, having never had just and adequate ideas of the evil of sin, or its consequences. We should also recollect how backward human nature is in forming spiritual ideas, and entering upon a holy self-denying conversation. We ought not, therefore, even after many falls, to give up and cast away a relapsed convert while he manifests the least inclination to be washed from his filthiness. (278)

The community also agreed to walk circumspectly around the converts, since their conduct would be a "specimen of what Christ looks for in His disciples" (279). Finally, the female members of the Serampore community would also be engaged in building relationships with the native women, in imitation of the pious women of the New Testament. To facilitate this, the women of the community would be assisted in learning the native language.

Eighth, the community commits to the formation of native converts for the purpose of seeing Indians win other Indians for Jesus Christ. The Serampore missionaries understood the great obstacles that hindered Europeans from evangelizing the continent of India, so they imagined that the best way to do so was to raise up an army of native missionaries. The first step in this process was to "advise the native brethren who may be formed in separate churches, to choose their pastors and deacons from amongst their own countrymen, that the word may be steadily preached, and the ordinances of Christ administered, in each church by the native minister" (280). A European missionary would continue to superintend the affairs of these native missionaries, but would do so in a way as to be as unobtrusive as possible. The end result of this organization is that there would be missionaries assigned to a number of mission centers, all under the oversight of a central missionary. As it turns out, this design is similar to the administrative arrangement of the Cluniac monasteries of the Middle Ages. The abbey of Cluny, founded in 910, became a very successful and prosperous monastery. Known for its rigorism and adherence to the Rule of Benedict, the monastery was soon asked to send monks to other monasteries in order to reform the laxity of observance of the rule. Cluny itself founded many new monasteries around the European continent. At its height, Cluny had hundreds of monasteries under its authority and governance, resulting in an administrative arrangement that saw the prior of Cluny as the titular head of all Cluniac monasteries. In theory, all Cluniac houses answered to the prior of Cluny. It seems that Carey and the other Serampore missionaries envisioned something similar.

Ninth, the members of the Serampore Mission committed themselves to learning the native languages and making translations of the Scriptures: "We consider the publication of the Divine Word throughout India as an object which we ought never to give up till accomplished" (282). Religious literature, too, was produced in the vernacular languages and distributed freely. The community also committed themselves to establishing free schools such as those founded by the Marshmans. Using schools to evangelize the Indians was seen as one of the most effective ways of creating a Christian nation.

Tenth, the community committed itself to prayer and "the cultivation of personal religion." The basis of this personal religion, states the Form of Agreement, is "Prayer—secret, fervent, believing prayer." Thus, prayer is seen as the foundation upon which the mission will be successful. To maintain community, even when separated, the members are admonished to "ever be united in prayer at stated seasons whatever distance may separate us" (283). This is similar to the injunction of the Rule of Benedict that stipulates that a monk on a journey away from the monastery who is unable to return to the oratory in time for communal prayer should "perform the Work of God where they are" (72.3). Moreover, "those who have been sent on a journey are not to omit the prescribed hours but to observe them as best they can" (72.4).

Eleventh, and lastly, the community is to commit themselves so fully to this ministry of evangelism that they are never to think of their time, gifts, strength, families, or even their clothes as their own. Everything belongs to God and they must seek to be sanctified for his work. Simply put, this item commits the community to possessing all things in common. The members agreed to "watch against a worldly spirit, and cultivate a Christian indifference towards every indulgence" (283–84).

Though unlike formal religious rules, the Form of Agreement does have a monastic spirit, particularly in its call to vigilant prayer and in its holding all possessions in common. Winter sees an even greater affinity with the monastic tradition when he notes that the three traditional vows of religious orders (poverty, chastity, and obedience) are evidenced in the writings of Carey and the Form of Agreement. The Serampore community's commitment to poverty is noted in their holding all things in common, not even counting their own clothes as their own. Their commitment to chastity did not entail celibacy, which is how it is often manifested in Roman Catholic religious orders, but their "necessary self-denial in the face of a crucial, urgent task."[68] Winter supports his contention with a quotation from Carey's *Enquiry*:

> A Christian minister is a person who in a peculiar sense is not his own; he is the servant of God, and therefore ought to be wholly devoted to him. By entering on that sacred office, he solemnly undertakes to be always engaged, as much as possible, in the Lord's work, and not to choose his own pleasure or employment, or pursue the ministry as a something that is to subserve his own ends or interests, or as a kind of by-work. He engages to go where God pleases, and to do or endure what he sees fit to command, or call him to, in the exercise of his function. He virtually bids farewell to friends, pleasures, and comforts, and stands in readiness to endure the greatest sufferings in the work of his Lord and Master.[69]

Thus, chastity manifests itself, for Winter, in Carey's general understanding of self-abnegation. Obedience at Serampore was manifested in the fact that no one was the self-appointed leader of the community. Winter describes the community as functioning with a "democracy of consensus" among its

---

68. Winter, "William Carey's Major Novelty," 211.
69. Ibid.

members. In short, though the Serampore Mission was not identical to a monastic order, it shared enough similarities with them that it is easy to see how the community could be thought of as a kind of monastic institution. This is supported by the fact that Carey seems to have read Millar's work, which included sections on the Roman Catholic religious orders. It would be wrong to state categorically that the Serampore Brotherhood was a "true" religious order, but as far as evangelical, Protestant history goes, it is one of the closest and the earliest monastic-like ventures. As well, it conforms nearly perfectly to Donald Bloesch's own idea of a Protestant religious center, thereby brining us full circle to the ongoing need of monasticism in today's evangelical, Protestant church.

Conclusion

It is my hope that having finished this volume, the reader is pleasantly surprised that not all Protestant authors have been against the institution of monasticism. Given the anemic state of historical rootedness in the larger landscape of evangelical Christendom, there is certainly a sense that most Protestants would be more tempted to throw the proverbial baby out with the bath water when it comes to monasticism, which has so often been seen as a uniquely Roman Catholic institution. In fact, that many Protestants have historically associated monasticism almost exclusively with the Roman Catholic Church and ignored its presence in the Eastern Orthodox churches demonstrates well the ahistorical nature of much evangelicalism.

For many in the evangelical world, monasticism, if it is considered at all, is perceived as a relic from the past, a retreat from the world, or a shirking from the call to the Great Commission. Few in the contemporary evangelical church have knowledge of the robust monastic tradition, the impetus for monastic vocation, the place of monasticism in the broader story of Christianity, or the real power and meaning of the monastic way of life. Thankfully, this situation is beginning to change. Contemporary evangelical spirituality possesses the desire for historical Christian manifestations of the faith. Younger evangelicals are hungry for more than they are getting spiritually; they seek and are calling for community, justice, and peace on the earth and authentic, transparent expressions of their Christian faith. A re-flourishing of historic monasticism, in principle if not in cenobitic practice, is just as important for the spiritual vitality of the evangelical church as the new monasticism mentioned above is for its social conscience. Monasticism was and is about love of God and union with him and, because of this fundamental commitment, it is still a vital force in the world and an important chapter in the history of the Christian church. As evangelicals continue to recover their tradition, they need to take seriously the role of monasticism and its contribution to the spiritual, intellectual, and institutional history of the Christian church. By doing this, as this book has tried to show, evangelicals will not be doing something new, but will be reinstituting what many Protestant authors had wanted all along—a monasticism that accords with the best of the Christian tradition and one that has its roots and motives firmly fixed in the Holy Scriptures.

BIBLIOGRAPHY

Allchin, A. M. *The Silent Rebellion: Anglican Religious Communities, 1845–1900.* London: SCM, 1958.

Anson, Peter F. *The Call of the Cloister: Religious Communities and Kindred Bodies in the Anglican Communion.* London: SPCK, 1955.

Armstrong, Chris. "The Monks Did It." Online: http://blog.christianitytoday.com/history/2009/05/the_monks_did_it.html.

Astell, Mary. *A Serious Proposal to the Ladies.* Edited by Patricia Springborg. Peterborough, ON: Broadview, 2002.

Atterbury, Francis. *Maxims, reflections and observations, divine, moral and political.* London, 1723.

Baker, James T. "Benedict's Children and Their Separated Brothers and Sisters." *The Christian Century*, December 3, 1980, 1191–94.

Barth, Karl. *The Christian Life: Church Dogmatics IV.4 Lecture Fragments.* Translated by Geoffrey W. Bromiley. Grand Rapids: Eerdmans, 1981.

———. *Church Dogmatics, Volume One: The Doctrine of the Word of God, Second Half-Volume.* Translated by G. T. Thomson and Harold Knight. New York: Scribner's, 1956.

———. *Church Dogmatics, Volume Four: The Doctrine of Reconciliation.* Translated by Geoffrey W. Bromiley. Edinburgh: T. & T. Clark, 1958.

———. *Church Dogmatics, Volume Three: The Doctrine of Creation.* Translated by A. T. Mackay, T. H. L. Parker, Harold Knight, Henry A. Kennedy, and John Marks. Edinburgh: T. & T. Clark, 1961.

———. *Ethics.* Edited by Dietrich Braun. Translated by Geoffrey W. Bromiley. New York: Seabury, 1981.

———. "Jesuiten und Klöster. Die umstrittenen Verbote in der Schweizerischen Bundesverfassung." *National-Zeitung* (Basel) 125.464 (1967) 1–2.

———. *Letters, 1961–1968.* Edited by Jürgen Fangmeier and Hinrich Stoevesandt. Translated and edited by Geoffrey W. Bromiley. Grand Rapids: Eerdmans, 1981.

———. *The Theology of John Calvin.* Translated by Geoffrey W. Bromiley. Grand Rapids: Eerdmans, 1995.

Beauregard, David. "Shakespeare on Monastic Life: Nuns and Friars in *Measure for Measure*." *Religion and the Arts* 5.3 (2001) 249–72.

Bibliography

Berkeley, George. *The Works of George Berkeley, D.D., Formerly Bishop of Cloyne.* Vol. 4, *Miscellaneous Works, 1707-50.* Oxford: Clarendon, 1901.

Bernard of Clairvaux. *Treatises I.* Spencer, MA: Cistercian, 1970.

Bessenecker, Scott A. *Living Mission: The Vision and Voices of New Friars.* Downers Grove, IL: InterVarsity, 2010.

Bethge, Eberhard. *Dietrich Bonhoeffer: Man of Vision, Man of Courage.* Translated by Eric Mosbacher et al. New York: Harper & Row, 1970.

"Biography: Rev. Sir George Wheler." *The Church of England Magazine* 8 (1840) 332-35.

Biot, François. *The Rise of Protestant Monasticism.* Translated by W. J. Kerrigan. Baltimore: Helicon, 1963.

Bloesch, Donald G. *Centers of Christian Renewal.* Philadelphia: United Church Press, 1964.

———. *The Christian Life and Salvation.* Grand Rapids: Eerdmans, 1967.

———. "The Christian Life in the Plan of Salvation." *Theology and Life* 5.4 (1962) 299-308.

———. *The Church: Sacraments, Worship, Ministry, Mission.* Downers Grove, IL: InterVarsity, 2002.

———. *The Crisis of Piety: Essays Towards a Theology of the Christian Life.* Grand Rapids: Eerdmans, 1968.

———. *The Future of Evangelical Christianity: A Call for Unity Amid Diversity.* Garden City, NY: Doubleday, 1983.

———. *Jesus Christ: Savior and Lord.* Downers Grove, IL: InterVarsity, 1997.

———. *The Struggle of Prayer.* San Francisco: Harper & Row, 1980.

———. *Wellsprings of Renewal: Promise in Christian Communal Life.* Grand Rapids: Eerdmans, 1974.

Bonhoeffer, Dietrich. *Discipleship.* Edited by Geffrey B. Kelly and John D. Godsey. Translated by Barbara Green and Reinhard Krauss. Minneapolis: Fortress, 2001.

———. *Life Together.* Translated by John W. Doberstein. New York: Harper & Row, 1954.

———. *London, 1933-1935.* Edited by Keith W. Clements. Minneapolis: Fortress, 2007.

———. *A Testament to Freedom: The Essential Writings of Dietrich Bonhoeffer.* Edited by Geffrey B. Kelly and F. Burton Nelson. Rev. ed. San Francisco: HarperSanFrancisco, 1995.

———. *The Way to Freedom: 1935-1939, from the Collected Works of Dietrich Bonhoeffer.* Edited by Edwin H. Robertson. Translated by Edwin H. Robertson and John Bowden. New York: Harper & Row, 1966.

Boulton, Matthew Myer. *Life in God: John Calvin, Practical Formation, and the Future of Protestant Theology.* Grand Rapids: Eerdmans, 2011.

Braght, Thieleman J. van. *The Bloody Theater, or, Martyr's Mirror.* Scottdale, PA: Herald, 1987.

Bramhall, John. *The Works of the Most Reverend Father in God, John Bramhall, D.D.* Vol. 1. Oxford: John Henry Parker, 1842.

Burke, Edmund. *Reflections on the Revolution in France.* Edited by L. G. Mitchell. Oxford: Oxford University Press, 1993.

Burnet, Gilbert. *Bishop Burnet's History of His Own Time from the Restoration of Charles II to the Treaty of Peace at Utrecht, in the Reign of Queen Anne.* Vol. 2. London: William Smith, 1840.

Burton, Robert. *The Anatomy of Melancholy.* Vol. 3. Edited by A. R. Shilleto. London: G. Bell, 1920.

Bibliography

Busch, Eberhard. "Barth, Karl." In *The Encyclopedia of Christianity*, edited by Erwin Fahlbusch et al., translated by Geoffrey W. Bromiley, 1:208–10. Grand Rapids: Eerdmans, 1999.

———. *Karl Barth and the Pietists: The Young Karl Barth's Critique of Pietism and Its Response*. Translated by Daniel W. Bloesch. Downers Grove, IL: InterVarsity, 2004.

Calvin, John. *Institutes of the Christian Religion*. Edited by John T. McNeill. Translated by Ford Lewis Battles. 2 vols. Philadelphia: Westminster, 1960.

"Carey Recommends Monastic Life." *The Christian Century*, December 15, 1999, 1220–21.

Carey, William. *An Enquiry into the Obligations of Christians, to Use Means of Conversion of the Heathens*. Leicester, 1792. Online: http://www.wmcarey.edu/carey/enquiry/anenquiry.pdf.

Carlstadt, Andreas Rudolff-Bodenstein von. *The Essential Carlstadt: Fifteen Tracts*. Translated and edited by E. J. Furcha. Scottdale, PA: Herald, 1995.

Carter, Erik. "The New Monasticism: A Literary Introduction." *Journal of Spiritual Formation and Soul Care* 5.2 (2012) 268–84.

Carter, J. F. M. *Nicholas Ferrar: His Household and His Friends*. Edited by T. T. Carter. London: Longmans, Green, 1892.

Clapp, Rodney. "Remonking the Church." *Christianity Today*, August 12, 1988, 20–21.

Clarke, Adam. *Memoirs of the Wesley Family; Collected Principally from Original Documents*. 2nd ed. New York: Lane & Tippett, 1848.

Cochrane, Arthur C. *Reformed Confessions of the Sixteenth Century*. Philadelphia: Westminster, 1966.

Cosin, John. *The Correspondence of John Cosin, D. D., Lord Bishop of Durham*. Part II. Durham: Andrews, 1872.

Cox, R. David. "Newman, Littlemore, and a Tractarian Attempt at Community." *Anglican and Episcopal History* 62.3 (1993) 343–76.

Crosthwaite, John Clark. *Modern Hagiology: An Examination of the Nature and Tendency of Some Legendary and Devotional Works lately Published under the Sanction of Rev. J. H. Newman, the Rev. Dr. Pusey, and the Rev. F. Oakeley*. Vol. 1. London: John W. Parker, 1846.

Dallas, Alexander R. C. *Protestant Sisters of Charity: A Letter Addressed to the Lord Bishop of London*. London: C. Knight, 1826.

Davis, Kenneth Ronald. *Anabaptism and Asceticism: A Study in Intellectual Origins*. Scottdale, PA: Herald, 1974.

Defoe, Daniel. *The Protestant Monastery; or, A Complaint against the Brutality of the Present Age*. London: W. Meadows, 1727.

Duncon, John. *Lady Lettice, Vi-Countess Falkland*. Edited by M. F. Howard. London: J. Murray, 1908.

Edwards, Jonathan. *The Religious Affections*. Carlisle, PA: Banner of Truth Trust, 2001.

Evelyn, John. *Diary and Correspondence of John Evelyn, F. R. S.* Edited by William Bray. Vol. 3. London: Henry Colburn, 1852.

———. *The Life of Mrs. Godolphin by John Evelyn of Wootton Esq*. Edited by Edward William Harcourt. London: Sampson Low, Marston, Searle, & Rivington, 1888.

Faught, C. Brad. *The Oxford Movement: A Thematic History of the Tractarians and Their Times*. University Park: Pennsylvania State University Press, 2003.

Froude, Richard Hurrell. *Remains of the Late Reverend Richard Hurrell Froude*. Vol. 1. London: Rivington, 1838.

Bibliography

Gelpi, Barbara Charlesworth. "John Keble and Hurrell Froude in Pastoral Dialogue." *Victorian Poetry* 44.1 (2006) 7–24.

Halkenhäuser, Johannes. *Kirche und Kommunität: Ein Beitrag zur Geschichte und zum Auftrag der kommunitären Bewegung in den Kirchen der Reformation.* Konfessionskundliche und Kontroverstheologische Studien 42. Paderborn: Bonifacius-Druckerei, 1978.

Harrison, J. F. C. *The Second Coming: Popular Millenarianism, 1780–1850.* New Brunswick: Rutgers University Press, 1979.

Hill, Bridget. "A Refuge from Men: The Idea of a Protestant Nunnery." *Past and Present* 117 (1987) 107–30.

Jaspert, Bernd. *Mönchtum und Protestantismus: Probleme und Wege der Forschung seit 1877.* Vol. 1, *Von Hermann Weingarten bis Heinrich Boehmer.* Regulae Benedicti Studia Supplementa 11. St. Ottilien: EOS, 2005.

———. *Mönchtum und Protestantismus: Probleme und Wege der Forschung seit 1877.* Vol. 2, *Von Karl Heussi bis Karl Barth.* Regulae Benedicti Studia Supplementa 15. St. Ottilien: EOS, 2006.

———. *Mönchtum und Protestantismus: Probleme und Wege der Forschung seit 1877.* Vol. 3, *Von Karlmann Beyschlag bis Martin Tetz.* Regulae Benedicti Studia Supplementa 19. St. Ottilien: EOS, 2007.

Keble, John. "Women Labouring in the Lord: A Sermon Preached at Wantage, on St. Mary Magdalene's Day, July 22, 1863." Oxford and London: John Henry & James Parker, 1863.

Kenyon, Ruth. "The Social Aspect of the Catholic Revival." In *Northern Catholicism: Centenary Studies in the Oxford and Parallel Movements*, edited by N. P. Williams and Charles Harris, 367–97. London: SPCK, 1933.

Kittelson, James M. *Luther the Reformer: The Story of the Man and His Career.* Minneapolis: Augsburg, 1986.

Krey, Philip D., and Peter D. S. Krey, editors and translators. *Luther's Spirituality.* Mahwah, NJ: Paulist, 2007.

Law, William. *A Serious Call to a Devout and Holy Life: The Spirit of Love.* Edited by Paul G. Stanwood. New York: Paulist, 1978.

Lawless, George. *Augustine of Hippo and His Monastic Rule.* Oxford: Clarendon, 1987.

Legg, J. Wickham. *English Church Life from the Restoration to the Tractarian Movement.* London: Longmans, Green, 1914.

Lenton, Edward. "Letter to Sir Thomas Hetley." In *Memoirs of the Life of Mr. Nicholas Ferrar*, by Peter Peckard, 285–305. Cambridge: J. Archdeacon, 1790.

Liddon, Henry Parry. *Life of Edward Bouverie Pusey.* Vol. 2. London: Longmans, Green, 1893.

———. *Life of Edward Bouverie Pusey.* Vol. 3. London: Longmans, Green, 1894.

Luther, Martin. *Luther's Works.* Vol. 44, *The Christian in Society I.* Edited by James Atkinson. Philadelphia: Fortress, 1966.

———. *Luther's Works.* Vol. 48, *Letters I.* Edited and translated by Gottfried G. Krodel. Philadelphia: Fortress, 1963.

———. *The Signs of Christ's Coming, and of the Last Day.* Translated by Anonymous. 1661.

Marshman, John Clark. *The Life and Times of Carey, Marshman, and Ward: Embracing the History of the Serampore Mission.* Vol. 1. London : Longman, Brown, Green, Longmans & Roberts, 1859.

Maycock, A. L. *Nicholas Ferrar of Little Gidding.* Grand Rapids: Eerdmans, 1980.

Bibliography

Moll, Rob. "The New Monasticism." *Christianity Today*, September 2, 2005, 38–46. Online: http://www.christianitytoday.com/ct/2005/september/16.38.html.
Monkres, Peter R. "An Innovative Ministry for Surplus Clergy." *The Christian Century*, February 7–14, 1979, 146–51.
Montagu, Mary Wortley. *The Works of the Right Honourable Lady Mary Wortley Montagu: Including Her Correspondence, Poems, and Essays*. London: Richard Phillips, 1803.
Newman, John Henry. *Apologia pro sua vita: Being a History of My Religious Opinions*. London: Longman, Green, Longman, Roberts, Green, 1865.
———. "The Apostolical Christian." In *Sermons Bearing on Subjects of the Day*, 275–92. London: Longmans, Green, 1902.
———. *Correspondence of John Henry Newman with John Keble and Others, 1839–1845*. Edited at the Birmingham Oratory. London: Longmans, Green, 1917.
———. "Home Thoughts Abroad." *British Magazine* 9 (1836) 357–69.
———. "Indulgence in Religious Privileges." In *Sermons Bearing on Subjects of the Day*, 112–25. London: Longmans, Green, 1902.
———. "John Davison." *The British Critic, Quarterly Theological Review and Ecclesiastical Record* 31 (1842) 375–420.
———. *The Letters and Diaries of John Henry Newman*. Vol. 5, *Liberalism in Oxford, January 1835 to December 1836*. Edited by Ian Ker and Thomas Gornall. Oxford: Clarendon, 1981.
———. *The Letters and Diaries of John Henry Newman*. Vol. 7, *Editing the British Critic, January 1839–December 1840*. Edited by Gerard Tracey. Oxford: Clarendon, 1995.
———. *The Letters and Diaries of John Henry Newman*. Vol. 8, *Tract 90 and the Jerusalem Bishopric, January 1841–April 1842*. Edited by Gerard Tracey. Oxford: Clarendon, 1999.
———. "Letters on the Church of the Fathers." *British Magazine* 7 (1835) 662–68.
———. "Temporal Advantages." In *Parochial and Plain Sermons*, 7:58–73. London: Rivingtons, 1868.
O'Neill, Simeon Wilberforce. "An Inquiry after the Secondary Causes of Success in Christian Missions." *The Ecclesiastic* 27 (1865) 123–31.
Op 't Hof, Willem J. "Protestant Pietism and Medieval Monasticism." In *Confessionalism and Pietism: Religious Reform in Early Modern Europe*, edited by Fred van Lieburg, 31–50. Mainz: Philipp von Zabern, 2006.
Oussoren, A. H. *William Carey, Especially his Missionary Principles*. Leiden: A. W. Sijthoff, 1945.
Packer, J. I. *A Quest for Godliness: The Puritan Vision of the Christian Life*. Wheaton, IL: Crossway, 1990.
Parker, T. H. L. *John Calvin: A Biography*. Philadelphia: Westminster, 1975.
Pauley, John-Bede. "The Implication of Monastic Qualities on the Pastoral Provision for the 'Anglican Use.'" *Antiphon* 10.3 (2006) 261–76.
Peters, Greg. "Monasticism." In *The Dictionary of Christian Spirituality*, edited by Glen G. Scorgie, 618–20. Grand Rapids: Zondervan, 2011.
Pipkin, H. Wayne. "Zwingli, the Laity and the Orders: From the Cloister into the World." *Hartford Quarterly* 8 (1968) 32–41.
Plumptre, E. H. *The Life of Thomas Ken, D.D.* Vol 2. London: William Isbister, 1889.
"Protestant Sisters of Charity." *Blackwood's Edinburgh Magazine* 18 (July–December 1825) 732–35.

Bibliography

Richardson, Samuel. *The History of Sir Charles Grandison, Bart.* Vol. 4. London: Chapman & Hall, 1902.

———. *The History of Sir Charles Grandison, Bart.* Vol. 5. London: Chapman & Hall, 1902.

Rinderknecht, Jakob. "Discovering a Common Life: The Liturgy of the Hours in Lutheran Religious Communities." *American Benedictine Review* 62 (2011) 242–64.

"Romanist Saints and Tractarian Movements." *Christian Observer* 44 (1844) 559–75, 730–768.

Russell, George W. E. *The Household of Faith: Portraits and Essays.* 2nd ed. London: Hodder & Stoughton, 1903.

Russell, Robin. "Intentional Community: New Monasticism Encourages Disciplined Life." *The United Methodist Reporter*, September 9, 2011. Online: http://www.umportal.org/article.asp?id=5851.

Santos, Jason Brian. *A Community Called Taizé: A Story of Prayer, Worship and Reconciliation.* Downers Grove, IL: InterVarsity, 2008.

Schleiermacher, Friedrich. *On Religion: Speeches to Its Cultured Despiers.* Translated and edited by Richard Crouter. 2nd ed. Cambridge: Cambridge University Press, 1996.

School(s) for Conversion: Twelve Marks of a New Monasticism. Edited by The Rutba House. Eugene, OR: Cascade, 2005.

Schroeder, Carl J. *In Quest of Pentecost: Jodocus van Lodenstein and the Dutch Second Reformation.* Lanham, MD: University Press of America, 2001.

Sharp, Thomas. *Life of John Sharp, D.D., Lord Archbishop of York.* Vol. 2. London: C. & J. Rivington, 1825.

Shorthouse, Joseph Henry. *John Inglesant: A Romance.* 6th ed. New York: Macmillan, 1895.

Smith, A. Christopher. "A Tale of Many Models: The Missiological Significance of the Serampore Trio." *Missiology: An International Review* 20.4 (1992) 479–500.

Southey, Robert. *Sir Thomas More: Or, Colloquies on the Progress and Prospects of Society.* Vol. 2. London: John Murray, 1829.

Stephens, Edward. *Asceticks: or, The Heroick Piety and Virtue of the Ancient Christian Anchorets and Coenobites: Exemplary Asceticks.* London, 1696.

———. *A Letter to a Lady: Concerning the Due Improvement of Her Advantages of Celibacie, Portion, and Maturity of Age and Judgment: which May Serve Indifferently for Men Under the Same Circumstances.* London, 1695.

Stevenson, Robert Louis. *A Child's Garden of Verses and Underwoods.* New York: Current Literature, 1913.

———. *Travels with a Donkey in the Cevennes.* New York: Scribner's, 1903.

Thorndike, Herbert. *The Theological Works of Herbert Thorndike.* Vol. 5. Oxford: John Henry Parker, 1854.

Travers, Walter Joseph. *Autobiography of Father Bede of St. Simon Stock.* In *Carmel in England: A History of the English Mission of the Discalced Carmelites, 1615–1849,* 171–307. London: Burns & Oates, 1899.

Visioni attuali sulla vita monastica. Montserrat, 1966.

Webster, J. B. *Barth.* 2nd ed. London: Continuum, 2004.

Weiser, Frederick S. "Communal Ministries in Lutheranism: The Historical Precedent." *American Benedictine Review* 19 (1968) 301–16.

———. *The Survival of Monastic Life in Post-Reformation Lutheranism.* MST thesis, Lutheran Theological Seminary at Philadelphia, 1966.

Wendebourg, Dorothea. "Luther on Monasticism." In *The Pastoral Luther: Essays on Martin Luther's Practical Theology*, edited by Timothy J. Wengert, 327–54. Grand Rapids: Eerdmans, 2009.
Wheler, George. *The Protestant monastery: or, Christian oeconomicks: Containing directions for the religious conduct of a family.* 1698.
White, Joseph Blanco. *The Life of the Rev. Joseph Blanco White, Written by Himself; with Portions of His Correspondance.* Edited by John Hamilton. Vol. 2. London: John Chapman, 1845.
Wicklow, Earl of. "The Monastic Revival in the Anglican Communion." *Studies: An Irish Quarterly Review* 42 (1953) 420–32.
Williams, Thomas Jay. *Priscilla Lydia Sellon: The Restorer, after Three Centuries, of the Religious Life in the English Church.* London: SPCK, 1950.
Wilson-Hartgrove, Jonathan. *New Monasticism: What It Has to Say to Today's Church.* Grand Rapids: Brazos, 2008.
Winter, Ralph D. "William Carey's Major Novelty." *Missiology: An International Review* 22.2 (1994) 203–22.
Wordsworth, William. *The Complete Poetical Works of William Wordsworth.* London: Macmillan, 1888.
———. *Ecclesiastical Sonnets.* Online: http://www.everypoet.com/archive/poetry/William_Wordsworth/william_wordsworth_contents.htm.
———. *The Poetical Works of William Wordsworth.* Edited by William Knight. Vol. 3. London: Macmillan, 1896.
Youings, Joyce. *The Dissolution of the Monasteries.* London: Allen & Unwin, 1971.
Zeller, Winfried. "The Protestant Attitude to Monasticism, with Special Reference to Gerhard Tersteegen." *Downside Review* 93 (1975) 178–92.

INDEX

Adams, Richard, 7
Anabaptism, 5, 11
Anglican Communion, 17, 90
Anglicanism, 73, 74, 78
Annoni, Hieronymus, 92
Antony, 32–33
Aquinas, Thomas, 99
Arnold, Eberhard, 119
Astell, Mary, 59
Athanasius, 32, 61
Atterbury, Francis, 62
Augsburg Confession, 10, 120, 122
Augustine of Hippo, 37, 43, 44
Augustinians, 11, 34

Baker, James, 141–42
baptism, 11, 26–28, 34, 42–43, 46, 97–98, 111
Barth, Fritz, 91, 93
Barth, Karl, 17, 91–110, 111, 114, 125, 128, 140
Basil of Caesarea, 43, 96, 99, 101
Bell, George, 114
Benedict of Nursia, 51, 95, 99, 101, 119
Benedictine(s), 4–5, 10–11, 29, 34, 56, 70, 102, 104–6, 118, 124, 147
Benson, Richard Meux, 88–90
Berkeley, George, 64
Bernard of Clairvaux, 6, 12, 29–30, 37
Bernhardi, Bartholomew, 24

Bessenecker, Scott, 144
Bethge, Eberhard, 115
Biot, François, 17
Blackwood's Edinburgh Magazine, 9, 64
Bloesch, Donald, 14, 17, 127–40, 152
Blomfield, Charles, 83
Bodenstein von Carlstadt, Andreas, 50–51
Bonhoeffer, Dietrich, 17, 110–20, 125
Böni, Josef, 108–9
Boulton, Matthew, 39, 47–48
Bowden, Caroline, 66
Bowden, J. H., 80
Boyle, Robert, 58
Bramhall, John, 55–56
Brasó, Gabriel M., 104–5
Breit, Peter, 11
Bruce, Mary, 84
Brunner, Emil, 128
Bullinger, Heinrich, 91
Bultmann, Rudolph, 128
Bunyan, John, 8, 101
Burckhardt, Johann, 92
Burke, Edmund, 54
Burnet, Gilbert, 62
Burton, Robert, 57–58
Busch, Eberhard, 91–94

Calvin, John, 17, 19, 38–48, 49, 51, 91, 95, 130
Carey, George, 13–14, 16

163

Index

Carey, William, 144–48, 150–52
Carthusians, 8, 58
Cavendish, Margaret, 6, 59
celibacy, 7, 11, 12, 14, 24, 26, 27, 35, 37, 41, 46, 49, 51, 56, 57, 67, 71, 72, 75, 89, 121, 123, 132, 133, 139–49, 151
Chamberlain, Thomas, 81
Chamberlayne, Edward, 59
Chambers, Catherine, 85
Christian Year, The, 68, 72
Christianity Today, 15, 16, 141
Chrysostom, John, 43
Church Dogmatics, 17, 91, 92, 94, 95, 97, 98, 99–100, 105–7, 109
Churton, E., 80
Cistercian(s), 1, 6, 10, 11, 12, 20, 29, 30
Claiborne, Shane, 15
Clapp, Rodney, 142
Cluniac, monastery, 150
Collège de la Marche, 38
Collège de Montaigu, 38
Commentary on True and False Religion, 49
common ownership, 12, 124
Confessing Church, 91, 110–11, 113, 120
confession, 34, 38, 67, 68, 92, 94, 111–12, 115, 116, 119, 138
Convent of Pleasure, The. See Cavendish, Margaret
Cooke, James, 144
Cost of Discipleship, 111, 115
Cox, R. David, 67
Cranmer, Thomas, 63
Cromwell, Thomas, 53
Crosthwaite, John, 79
Cuningham, William, 63–64

Dallas, Alexander, 65
Davenant, John, 6–7
Davies, Myles, 9
Davison, John, 76–77
de Acosta, Jose, 147
de Nobili, Roberto, 147
deaconesses, 45–46, 123–24

Defoe, Daniel, 62, 64
Dodsworth, William, 83, 84
Dominican(s), 6, 34, 144
Duncon, John, 57

Edwards, Jonathan, 13
Ellacombe, Henry Thomas, 84
Ellacombe, Jane, 84
England, 5, 8, 11, 12, 13, 15, 16, 53, 54, 55, 56, 60, 61, 62, 63, 66, 67, 68, 69, 70, 71, 72, 73, 74, 76, 78, 79, 80, 81, 83, 84, 85, 86, 87, 88, 89, 114, 144
Eucharist, 98, 124, 125
evangelism, 7, 135, 136, 138, 139, 151
Expositions and Proof of the Articles. See "Sixty-Seven Articles, The"
Evelyn, John, 58–59

Faber, John, 48
faith, 7, 11, 20–22, 27–31, 33–35, 51, 79, 86, 92–94, 98, 104, 121, 125, 130, 133, 135, 138, 140, 149, 153
Falkland, Lettice, 57
Farel, William, 38
fasting, 22, 23, 43, 46, 74, 75, 78
Faught, C. Brad, 66–67
Ferrar family, 54–55, 57, 72
Fliedner, Theodor, 123
Francis of Assisi 95, 101
Franciscan(s), 5, 6, 11, 34, 144
freedom, 10, 20, 21, 25, 31–32, 34, 43, 61, 64, 92, 96, 102, 109, 124, 139
Freedom of a Christian, The, 20–23, 28
Froude, Richard Hurrell, 16, 66, 67, 71–72, 73, 79
Fuller, Andrew, 144
Fuller, Thomas, 58
Future of Evangelical Christianity, The, 132

Gelpi, Barbara, 72
Gelzer, Charlotte, 93

Index

Germany, 10, 11, 79, 93, 110, 113, 114, 120, 123, 124, 125, 129
Ghandi, Mahatma, 114
Gladstone, William, 79
Godolphin, Elizabeth, 59
Gollwitzer, Helmuth, 110
Gottschalk, Heino, 10
Grafton, Charles, 88–89
Gregory of Nazianzus, 43
Guldin, Nikolaus, 11

Hall, Joseph, 6
Harrison, J. F. C., 12
Hartshorne, Charles, 128
Helt, Conrad, 24
Henry VIII, 11, 14, 53, 55, 62, 69
Herrmann, Wilhelm, 91
Hetley, Thomas, 55
Hitler, Adolph, 110
holiness, 21, 33–35, 48, 54, 94, 98, 130–32, 135, 142, 148
Holl, Karl, 107
Hughes, Marion, 81–82

Institutes of the Christian Religion, 38, 39
Iona, monastery, 14

James, John, 64
Jesuits, 109–110
Judgment of Martin Luther on Monastic Vows, The, 20, 24
justice, 14, 41, 66, 127, 153
justification, 20–24, 28, 30–31, 51, 93, 98, 104, 121, 130–31, 138–39

Keble, John, 66–69, 71–72, 73, 78, 79, 80, 88
Ken, Thomas, 57
Kenyon, Ruth, 67
Kierkegaard, Soren, 128

Lambarde, William, 6
Lamm, Theophil, 124
Langston, Emma, 84
Lauterburg, Otto, 108
Lee, Ann, 12

Leich, Werner, 125
Lenton, Edward, 55
Life Together, 111, 113, 114, 116, 119, 120
Loehe, William, 123–24
Loyola, Ignatius, 101
Luther, Martin, 8, 10, 17, 19–37, 39, 46, 47, 48, 49, 50, 51, 95, 96, 107, 108, 112, 113, 120, 121, 122, 124, 130, 132, 135
Law, William, 64

Macarius the Great, 101
Mackarness, John, 89
MacLeod, George F., 14
Madauss, Erica, 124–125
Manners, John, 83
marriage, 9, 28, 41, 46, 49, 57, 59, 72, 75, 81, 96, 123, 124, 139–40
Marshman, Joshua, 145
Maycock, A. L., 55
meditation, 61, 78, 119–20, 133, 141
Melanchthon, Philip, 24, 121
Meland, Bernard, 128
Milton, John, 6
Moll, Rob, 142
monasticism
    criticism of, 1–10
    dissolution of the monasteries, 14, 53, 55, 62, 65
    etymology of, 101
    vows, 5, 7, 8, 10, 11, 16, 23, 24–32, 34–37, 39–51, 55, 62–65, 81, 89, 102, 121, 124, 132, 151
Monkres, Peter, 140–42
Montagu, Mary Wortley, 59–60
More, Thomas, 65
Moses, 50
Mozley, Jemima, 74
Mozley, Thomas, 73

"National Apostasy," 73
National Socialism, 91, 92
New Friars, 15, 144
New Monasticism, 15–16, 113, 142–44, 153

165

Index

Newman, John Henry, 16, 17, 67, 68, 71, 72, 73–79, 80, 81, 84
Nicholls, William, 9
Niebuhr, Reinhold, 128

O'Neill, Simeon Wilberforce, 88, 89
obedience, 5, 10, 11, 14, 25, 35, 36, 37, 39, 46, 49, 50, 55, 81, 89, 98, 106, 112, 113, 121, 123, 124, 125, 132, 141, 151
On Monastic Vows, 20, 24, 25, 26, 32, 34
Oriel College, 68, 71, 73, 76, 79, 84
Oxford Movement, 66, 67, 68, 71, 72, 73, 76, 79
Oxford University, 9, 16, 17, 57, 66, 68, 79, 129

Paphnutius, 33
Pauck, Wilhelm, 128
Paul, apostle, 5, 7, 27, 29, 30, 31, 32, 35, 44, 46, 77, 79, 107, 148
Pelikan, Jaroslav, 128
penance, 10, 23, 28, 74, 76
perfection, 7, 22, 27, 44, 56, 58, 61, 64, 76, 78, 81, 88, 99, 138
pharisaism, 129, 131, 132
Pharisees, 6, 7
Phillpotts, Henry, 84–85
Pietists, 17, 93, 133
poverty, 5, 8, 10, 12, 14, 25, 44, 49, 55, 64, 75, 76, 81, 89, 102, 121, 123, 132, 139, 141, 144, 151
Prescott, Oliver, 88
Reformation, Protestant, 4, 5, 10, 11, 13, 14, 16, 17, 44, 56, 58, 60, 62, 65, 69, 70, 71, 76, 80, 90, 93, 95, 96, 100, 107, 108, 109, 112, 120, 121, 124, 130, 133, 134, 148
psalms, 20, 39, 47, 48, 78, 117, 119, 120
Psalter, 117
Puritanism, 7
Puritans, 7, 55, 148
Pusey, Edward, 67, 68, 72, 74, 76, 79–85, 87, 88

Pusey, Lucy, 81, 83

Quaker(s), 12, 148

Reflections on the Revolution in France. See Burke, Edmund
Reidinger, Paul, 125
Remains. See Froude, Richard Hurrell
repentance, 30, 42, 111, 118, 125
Richardson, Samuel, 64
righteousness, 13, 20, 21, 22, 31, 39, 43, 98, 130, 131
Roman Catholicism, 56, 60, 64, 67, 73, 74, 76, 79, 139, 147
Rule of St. Benedict, 11, 29, 56, 99, 119, 120, 124, 125, 150

salvation, 6, 10, 19, 20, 21, 22, 23, 29, 30, 31, 34, 56, 116, 117, 127, 129, 130, 131, 132, 133, 139, 140, 148, 149
Sancroft, William, 56
Sattler, Michael, 4–5
Schiemer, Leonhard, 5
Schleiermacher, Freidrich, 4, 92
Schlink, Klara, 124–25
Schroeder, Carl, 12–13
Schütz-Marsauche, Roger Louis, 14
Seager, Charles, 81–82
self-righteousness, 133
Sellon, Priscilla Lydia, 84–87
Serampore Brotherhood, 146–47, 152
Serampore Mission, 145–47, 150, 152
Serious Proposal to the Ladies, A, 59
service, 15, 25, 39, 42, 60, 70, 76, 81, 82, 84, 104, 105, 106, 115, 119, 131, 132, 135, 137, 139, 140, 142
Shakers, 12
Shakespeare, William, 11–12
Sharp, Thomas, 63–64
Shorthouse, Joseph Henry, 54
"Sixty-Seven Articles, The," 49
solitude, 6, 54, 118, 119, 120, 133, 140, 142
Southey, Robert, 65–66, 83
Spalatin, George, 24

Index

Standonck, Jean, 38
Stephens, Edward, 60–61
Stevenson, Robert Louis, 1–4
Struggle of Prayer, The, 131
Sutz, Erwin, 114
Synod of Barmen, 92

Taizé, monastery, 14
Terrot, Sarah, 85
Tersteegen, Gerhard, 17, 92–94
Tertullian, 62
Theology of John Calvin, 108
Theresa of Ávila, 101
Thomas, à Kempis, 12, 99, 101
Thorndike, Herbert, 56–57
Tillich, Paul, 128
Tillotson, John, 61
Tractarianism. *See* Oxford Movement
"Tracts for the Times," 68, 73
Turnbull, Bertha, 87
Tyndale, William, 5–6

University of Basel, 92
University of Bonn, 92
University of Erfurt, 19
University of Paris, 38
University of Wittenberg, 20, 50

van Lodenstein, Jodocus, 12–13, 16
von Harnack, Adolf, 91

von Rohden, L., 92
von Zinzendorf, Nicholas, 92

Ward, William, 145, 148
Webster, John, 92
Wendebourg, Dorothea, 11
Wesley, John, 62, 148
Wesley, Samuel, 62–63
Wheler, George, 60
White, Joseph Blanco, 78
Whitefield, George, 149
widows, 35, 45, 46, 54, 57
Wilberforce, Samuel, 89
Williams, Daniel Day, 128
Wilson-Hartgrove, Jonathan, 15, 143
Winter, Ralph, 146, 147, 151
Wood, S. F., 74
Wordsworth, William, 69–70, 85–86
works, 6, 21, 22, 23, 28, 29, 30, 31, 34, 35, 39, 51, 76, 86, 87, 103, 129, 130, 132
works-righteousness, 19, 129, 130
worship, 8, 39, 40, 44, 45, 47, 51, 61, 63, 103, 109, 110, 114, 118, 121, 122, 123, 124, 138, 142, 145, 147, 148

Xavier, Francis, 147

Zwingli, Ulrich, 9–10, 48–50, 51

www.ingramcontent.com/pod-product-compliance
Lightning Source LLC
Chambersburg PA
CBHW030856170426
43193CB00009BA/638